Teaching and Learning Third Languages

SECOND LANGUAGE ACQUISITION

Series Editors: **Professor David Singleton**, *University of Pannonia, Hungary* and Fellow Emeritus, *Trinity College, Dublin, Ireland* and **Professor Simone E. Pfenninger**, *University of Zurich, Switzerland*

This series brings together titles dealing with a variety of aspects of language acquisition and processing in situations where a language or languages other than the native language is involved. Second language is thus interpreted in its broadest possible sense. The volumes included in the series all offer in their different ways, on the one hand, exposition and discussion of empirical findings and, on the other, some degree of theoretical reflection. In this latter connection, no particular theoretical stance is privileged in the series; nor is any relevant perspective – sociolinguistic, psycholinguistic, neurolinguistic, etc. – deemed out of place. The intended readership of the series includes final-year undergraduates working on second language acquisition projects, postgraduate students involved in second language acquisition research, and researchers, teachers and policymakers in general whose interests include a second language acquisition component.

All books in this series are externally peer-reviewed.

Full details of all the books in this series and of all our other publications can be found on http://www.multilingual-matters.com, or by writing to Multilingual Matters, BLOCK, The Fairfax, Pithay Court, Bristol, BS1 3BN, UK.

SECOND LANGUAGE ACQUISITION: 159

Teaching and Learning Third Languages

Francesca D'Angelo

MULTILINGUAL MATTERS
Bristol • Jackson

DOI https://doi.org/10.21832/DANGEL3078
Library of Congress Cataloging in Publication Data
A catalog record for this book is available from the Library of Congress.
Names: D'Angelo, Francesca, author.
Title: Teaching and Learning Third Languages/Francesca D'Angelo.
Description: Bristol; Jackson, TN: Multilingual Matters, [2023] | Series: Second Language Acquisition: 159 | Includes bibliographical references and index. | Summary: "Contributing to emerging research on third language acquisition, this book presents readers with a practical guide to understanding how these languages are processed, learned and taught. With examples from a range of learning contexts, it emphasises the role of teachers as bridges between education and research on multilingualism"— Provided by publisher.
Identifiers: LCCN 2022052094 (print) | LCCN 2022052095 (ebook) | ISBN 9781800413078 (hardback) | ISBN 9781800413085 (pdf) | ISBN 9781800413092 (epub)
Subjects: LCSH: Language acquisition. | Language and languages—Study and teaching. | Multilingualism. Classification: LCC P118.15 .D36 2023 (print) | LCC P118.15 (ebook) | DDC 418.0071—dc23/eng/20230206
LC record available at https://lccn.loc.gov/2022052094
LC ebook record available at https://lccn.loc.gov/2022052095

British Library Cataloguing in Publication Data
A catalogue entry for this book is available from the British Library.

ISBN-13: 978-1-80041-307-8 (hbk)
ISBN-13: 978-1-83668-150-2 (pbk)

Multilingual Matters
UK: BLOCK, The Fairfax, Pithay Court, Bristol, BS1 3BN, UK.
USA: Ingram, Jackson, TN, USA.
Authorised Representative: Easy Access System Europe – Mustamäe tee 50, 10621 Tallinn, Estonia gpsr.requests@easproject.com.

Website: www.multilingual-matters.com
Bluesky: https://bsky.app/profile/multi-ling-mat.bsky.social
Twitter: Multi_Ling_Mat
Facebook: https://www.facebook.com/multilingualmatters
Blog: www.channelviewpublications.wordpress.com

Copyright © 2023 Francesca D'Angelo.

All rights reserved. No part of this work may be reproduced in any form or by any means without permission in writing from the publisher.

The policy of Multilingual Matters/Channel View Publications is to use papers that are natural, renewable and recyclable products, made from wood grown in sustainable forests. In the manufacturing process of our books, and to further support our policy, preference is given to printers that have FSC and PEFC Chain of Custody certification. The FSC and/or PEFC logos will appear on those books where full certification has been granted to the printer concerned.

Typeset by Deanta Global Publishing Services, Chennai, India.

A mia madre e mio padre:

per avermi insegnato la più preziosa delle lingue

Contents

Acknowledgements		xi
Introduction		1
1	Second vs Third Language Acquisition	6
	1.1 Introduction	6
	1.2 Third Language Acquisition	7
	1.3 The Benefits of Language Learning and the Bilingual Paradox	7
	1.4 The Holistic Approach beyond Bilingual and Monolingual Systems	9
	1.5 SLA vs TLA: Cognitive and Linguistic Differences	12
	1.6 Monolingual, Bilingual and Multilingual Speech Production Models	15
	1.7 Formal Approaches to Multilingual Acquisition: Crosslinguistic Influence in Third Language Acquisition	19
	1.8 Grosjean's Language Mode Hypothesis	25
	1.9 The Factor Model: L3/Ln Acquisition in Instructed Contexts	26
	1.10 The Multilingual Processing Model	27
	1.11 The Dynamic Model of Multilingualism	28
	1.12 No Boundaries Approach	30
	1.13 Interface Hypothesis	30
	1.14 Conclusion	32
2	The Role of Prior Formal Language Learning and Mediating Factors in Third or Additional Language Acquisition	33
	2.1 Introduction	33
	2.2 Attitudes towards Bilingualism: A Historical Perspective	33
	2.3 Bilingual Effects on Cognition and Language Learning: From Representation Analysis to Attentional Control	35
	2.4 Individual Learner Differences Affecting TLA	37

	2.5	The 'Bilingual Advantage' in Third Language Acquisition	43
	2.6	Level of Bilingualism: The Role of Proficiency in L3 Learning Performance	44
	2.7	Implicit and Explicit Language Learning and Knowledge	46
	2.8	The Role of Literacy in Prior Languages	51
	2.9	Early and Late Bilingualism: The Role of Age of Acquisition of Previous Languages	53
	2.10	Conclusion	54
3	Metalinguistic Awareness and Third or Additional Language Acquisition		56
	3.1	Introduction	56
	3.2	Defining Metalinguistic Awareness	57
	3.3	MLA and the Development of Multilingual Competence	59
	3.4	From Metalinguistic Knowledge to Metalinguistic Awareness	63
	3.5	Implicit and Explicit Metalinguistic Awareness and Language Learning	65
	3.6	The Role of Language Use and Language Knowledge in Third Language Acquisition	67
	3.7	Other Factors Affecting the Development of Metalinguistic Awareness: Schooling and Literacy	69
	3.8	Strategies to Develop Metalinguistic Awareness	71
	3.9	Learning Strategies and Cognitive Development	75
	3.10	Conclusion	77
4	Multilingual Education and Translanguaging: A 'Practical Theory of Languages'		79
	4.1	Introduction	79
	4.2	Multilingual Repertoire: Soft Boundaries between Linguistic Systems	79
	4.3	Translanguaging and Minority Languages	84
	4.4	The Monolingual Bias in Language Education Research	87
	4.5	Heritage Language Education: A Focus on Identity	88
	4.6	Translanguaging and Bilingual Education	89
	4.7	Unitary vs Crosslinguistic Translanguaging Orientations: A Theoretical Debate	96
	4.8	Conclusion	98
5	From Bilingual to Multilingual Education: Teaching, Assessing and Testing Trends		101
	5.1	Introduction	101
	5.2	The Monolingual and Bilingual Bias in Multilingual Testing and Assessment	102

5.3	Assessing Multilinguals: The Language Experience and Proficiency Questionnaire	107
5.4	Multilingual Teachers and Plurilingual Approaches	108
5.5	Training Multilingual Teachers	111
5.6	Teachers as 'Knowledge Generators': Crosslinguistic and Identity Practices	113
5.7	Translanguaging: The Teachers' Perspective	117
5.8	Inspiring Instructional Practices	120
5.9	Conclusion	124

Conclusion	126
References	130
Index	146

Acknowledgements

I am grateful to all those people I encountered on my path for inspiring and encouraging me to start, persevere with and publish the work. I thank all the teachers that made me the curious and passionate language learner, teacher and researcher I am today. I am immensely grateful to Oriana Palusci for being an excellent guidance: her continuous support, singular point of view and precious advice contributed to make me grow both as an individual and as a researcher. I would like to thank Antonella Sorace for introducing me to the fascinating world of cognitive linguistics, for her invaluable inspiration and for making my stay at the University of Edinburgh the best academic and personal experience I have ever had. I thank my lovely family for bearing with my long absences and distracted presences throughout the entire venture.

Introduction

This book is intended as an introduction for language learners, teachers, postgraduate students and researchers interested in exploring the phenomenon of teaching and learning third or additional languages from a bilingualist, cross-disciplinary perspective, i.e. cognitive, linguistic, affective and educational. It aims to analyse different nuances of multilingual education, highlighting its complexity and the wide range of individual and external factors characterising and affecting the phenomenon. Firstly, the work contributes to the research area of third or additional language acquisition (TLA) by advancing the theoretical framework considering it as a different field of study from second language acquisition (SLA) with a particular focus on the unique linguistic and cognitive profile of bilingual learners. Secondly, the book transcends the dichotomous conception of monolingualism and bilingualism, by addressing various forms and degrees of bilingualism and bilingual education theories and practices. Thirdly, from an educational point of view, it propounds a holistic perspective which focuses on the whole linguistic background of bilingual learners, rather than on the target languages, to enhance and support them in the process of TLA. For clarity, the term 'multilingual' ('multi' = many) is used in the work as an umbrella term that includes 'bilingual' speakers and education ('bi' = two) and it also refers to other types of multilingual education with three or more languages (Cenoz, 2013). The European Commission's (2007: 6) general definition of multilingualism is 'the ability of societies, institutions, groups and individuals to engage, on a regular basis, with more than one language in their day-to-day lives'. In particular, when referring to two or more languages, 'multilingual' and 'bilingual' (i.e. education, speakers, contexts, processes, etc.) are used, indistinctively, as generic terms. When opposing, specifically, speakers, acquisition processes, educational contexts, etc., involving two languages on the one hand and more than two languages on the other, the terms are used in their specific meaning: 'bi' vs 'multi'.

The work investigates the potential benefits of different types and degrees of bilingualism on additional language acquisition considering the effects of multiple methods of instruction and the amount of exposure to each language, going beyond the monolingual/bilingual dichotomous approach. It provides an insight into the language learners' profile from a cognitive and linguistic point of view, to question the monolingual approach to additional language learning and to distinguish the processes of SLA and TLA. The book reviews the implicit and explicit routes of acquisition available to learners together with a critical discussion of how they affect the development of different types and degrees of metalinguistic awareness (MLA). In particular, it emphasises the concept of MLA as a cognitive element that 'can contribute to the catalytic or accelerating effect in TLA' (Jessner, 2008b: 26). Previous and current research which has so far provided evidence of positive correlations between MLA and multilingual competence (Bialystok & Barac, 2012; Cenoz, 2003; Cummins, 1979; Fehling, 2008; Jaensch, 2009) is reviewed to thoroughly understand the extent to which developing this cognitive skill is crucial to additional language learning.

An overview of the controversial discussion dealing with the non-unitary nature of MLA, which may be considered as both cognitive and linguistic, implicit and explicit, is provided (Bialystok, 2001; Cenoz, 2003; Rebuschat & Williams, 2012; Seel, 2012). Additionally, together with the paramount role it plays in additional language learning, the work also examines its mediating role, under a psycholinguistic perspective, between two areas of research that have generally overlooked each other, i.e. bilingualism and TLA. Different routes to develop and enhance MLA are propounded to create connections between languages and exploit the peculiar multilingual profile of language learners not only in terms of broader linguistic repertoire and linguistic skills but also in terms of learning strategies developed in previous languages.

The theoretical discussion, focusing on the most significant conceptual and empirical studies on multilingual education, going beyond the specificity of any context-based application, is reviewed to make the contents relevant to a wider variety of multilingual learners across different areas. Moreover, the book compares and integrates concepts and theories, referring to different dimensions of bilingualism, across the aforementioned implicit–explicit continuum. It questions and challenges the monolingual approach to additional language learning with empirical evidence from the cognitive linguistics field, comparing and contrasting innovative and inspiring learning and teaching practices which empower and engage multilingual students. The book proposes a flexible and adaptive framework for designing and implementing multilingual learning environments and strategies belonging to different approaches, namely crosslinguistic transfer and translanguaging, to provide a broader and comprehensive view of multilingual education across a variety of instructional settings. Thus, the book intends to promote linguistically based instruction programmes for bilinguals by providing evidence that formal instruction received in more than one language is conducive to higher levels of MLA. Considering that MLA represents one of the 'language learning and teaching goals', as defined by the *Common European Framework of Reference for Languages* (Council of Europe, 2001: 134), it is crucial to define and create the appropriate linguistic setting through innovative teaching practices, to develop and train this fundamental cognitive skill to fully exploit the benefits of bilingualism in multiple language acquisition.

Chapter 1 highlights the importance of considering SLA and TLA as two distinct processes for many linguistic, cognitive and affective reasons. It reviews and compares the principal speech production models advanced in SLA and in TLA from the field of psycholinguistics. The chapter discusses the reasons why a more comprehensive, holistic and interdisciplinary approach is needed to portray the complexity and variability of TLA due to its high number of internal and external factors. In the last two decades, due to the rise in multilingualism as an individual and social phenomenon, there has been a considerable increase in interest in the positive effects of bilingualism in TLA. Nonetheless, TLA was generally included either in the field of bilingualism or the field of SLA. Despite the similarities between TLA and SLA, the chapter contributes to supporting the view that the main difference deals with the cognitive and linguistic profile of the language learners involved. More specifically, in SLA learners are monolinguals at the initial stage of language learning whereas in TLA learners are already bilingual (Gonzàlez Alonso *et al.*, 2016; Grosjean, 1992). Moreover, it has been noticed that while in SLA there are only two possible routes to follow, i.e. simultaneous and consecutive acquisition, in TLA the number of routes increases substantially as there are at least four main types of order of acquisition (De Angelis, 2007).

Chapter 2 examines the impact of different mediating factors responsible for bilinguals' better performance when learning additional languages. The myths, common beliefs and empirical findings are analysed to disentangle the complex relationship between previously acquired languages and TLA. Specifically, the chapter reviews the benefits of having already learned a second language on learning another in terms of the transfer of knowledge, language abilities, learning strategies, vocabulary and sensitivity to grammatical differences, supported by a number of studies (Genesee & Lambert, 1983; Klein, 1995; Swain *et al.*, 1990; Thomas, 1988). Despite the increasing number of empirical studies on the cognitive and linguistic effects of bilingualism, the literature still shows no consensus on the main factors responsible for bilinguals' better performance when learning foreign languages. The chapter aims to compare and contrast previous and current research on TLA to determine the extent to which a number of cognitive and affective attributes have a significant impact on the performance of bilinguals when learning any additional language in a formal context. Among the individual learners' differences linked to previous language learning, it takes into account the potential effect of different types of learning, amount of exposure to any previous language, context and age of acquisition, level of bilingualism, literacy and attitude towards the languages.

Chapter 3 deals with research focused on the relationship between MLA and previous language learning experience. The aim is to analyse how these factors can be conceptualised, how they develop and in which way they may affect each other. Additionally, it investigates the non-unitary nature of MLA, which is difficult to assess experimentally and significantly influences the process and outcome of TLA. The evidence for it being both linguistic and cognitive, implicit and explicit, is discussed in an attempt to provide a complete overview of the multiple nuances that characterise this complex entity. Furthermore, the variables known to have an effect on its development, including different types of bilingualism, literacy and implicit or explicit instruction, are investigated to better understand its relevance in terms of multilingual education. A clarification of the terminology employed in previous and current research on metalinguistic concepts, i.e. metalinguistic knowledge and MLA, is provided. Chapter 3 further aims to disentangle the notion of attention from awareness, focusing on the cognitive aspect of the role played by MLA in additional language learning. Finally, it looks at the impact of different types of instruction settings on the development of MLA to highlight how language learning and MLA relate to each other.

Chapter 4 investigates different approaches to multilingualism and multilingual education which differ considerably in terms of the conceptualisation of languages, language boundaries and multilingual learners. The work deals with the theoretical debate dividing unitary and cross-linguistic translanguage theorists on the legitimacy of code-switching and additive bilingualism. It reviews a number of theories propounded by scholars from the formal approach and from the Dynamic System Theory. The first conceives languages as clearly circumscribed and transferable identities. The second puts forward the view that languages are dynamically integrated subsystems. However, the most interesting approach, in terms of the countability and delimitation of language varieties, comes from translanguaging, an innovative 'practical theory of languages' (Li, 2017), particularly suitable for the context of multilingual acquisition where learners' L1 is different from the official language of instruction. It can be conceived as a linguistic theory going beyond the countability of languages, conceived as unbounded, fluid and interwoven systems. Different social contexts where translanguaging is particularly advisable to enhance the multilingual repertoire of learners are described, including the diverse linguistic, cognitive and sociocultural backgrounds of learners. Additionally, a special focus of the chapter deals with how to implement translanguaging practices aimed at preserving and supporting minority and heritage languages and identities.

Chapter 5 explores the challenges of teaching, testing and assessing multilingual learners in different educational contexts. It discusses how multilingual testing and assessment have improved considerably in the last decades due to the higher level of attention devoted to this field of research. The change was determined by a number of sociolinguistic and educational factors including the perceived and acknowledged need of policymakers, researchers and educators to integrate immigrant students into mainstream education programmes. That is, it was necessary to adapt the assessment tools to the diverse variety of language backgrounds, educational contexts and geographic origins characterising multilingual classrooms. Nonetheless, despite the step forward compared to monolingual assessment practices, as De Angelis (2021) observes, most academic discussions still focus on speakers of two languages, including bilingual assessment and testing needs in homogeneous settings (i.e. balanced bilingualism). The chapter ends with a critical discussion of how the majority of testing material developed in the last decades has been tailored to the specific needs of bilingual speakers and learners and does not seem suitable to test and assess multilinguals. A number of crosslinguistic and translanguaging instructional practices, designed and implemented in different multilingual contexts, are propounded to inspire teachers to adopt more inclusive educational strategies aiming at exploiting the full multilingual and multicultural repertoire of learners.

1 Second vs Third Language Acquisition

1.1 Introduction

Multilingualism and multiculturalism are functional realities of contemporary societies. They challenge the way languages are conceived as well as the traditional visions of language education. The acknowledgement of the importance of bilingualism as an existing, *de facto*, reality has led to the development of different approaches, models, theories and pedagogical practices in the field of second language acquisition (SLA) research. Furthermore, the field of multilingual acquisition, learning, testing and assessment has grown considerably in recent years to meet the sociolinguistic needs of a multilingual, multicultural and multimodal world. The proliferation of studies on multilingualism, since the beginning of the 21st century, is due to the increasing number of multilinguals and the spread of modern foreign language learning (Ziegler, 2013). The increase in multilingualism may be the result of historical or political movements, migrations for economic reasons or the need to connect and communicate with wider areas of the world through the development of new communication media technologies.

Hence, models and theories developed by SLA researchers can no longer be employed to describe and analyse the process of language learning and the profile of multilingual speakers. Consequently, third (or additional) language acquisition (TLA) set itself as a new area of research to shed light on the differences with SLA in terms of processes of acquisition. Most importantly, TLA research switches the focus from the target language to the much more complex and diverse cognitive and linguistic profile of multilingual learners. Drawing on the cognitive and educational perspectives, this chapter discusses the benefits and challenges of processing and learning additional languages when bilingual learners are involved. It reviews and compares the principal speech production and crosslinguistic models advanced in SLA and TLA from the fields of psycholinguistics, discussing the reasons why a more comprehensive, holistic and interdisciplinary approach is needed to portray the complexity and variability of TLA due to the number of internal and external factors affecting the phenomenon.

1.2 Third Language Acquisition

TLA is a relatively new field of study that has developed considerably in the last decades. It refers to the study of a non-native language by learners who have previously acquired or are acquiring two languages. Cenoz (2013: 3) defines it as 'the acquisition of a language that is different from the first and second and is acquired after them'. Moreover, it is important to stress that the expression TLA refers to the acquisition of a third or additional language as well as the area of research itself. The study of TLA brings together two fields of study that have traditionally overlooked each other, that is, SLA and the study of the effects of bilingualism on the other. Despite the similarities between SLA and TLA, it can be argued that there are a number of reasons to consider TLA as a distinct process and area of research from SLA. Indeed, the rise of TLA in the last few decades has been considered a reaction to the neglect of its differences with SLA. What mostly differentiates the two processes, generally speaking, is the greater language experience that third language (L3) learners have at their disposal, the general effects of bilingualism on cognition and the access to two linguistic systems when acquiring an additional language.

This chapter deals with two main aspects that have received attention in studies on TLA. Firstly, the difference between monolingual and bilingual speech processing and language acquisition modes, reviewing the most influential models put forward by academics in the last decades. Secondly, the analysis of different study approaches to multilingual language acquisition is characterised by different methodologies and different degrees of formalisation. Formal approaches to the acquisition of syntax and morphosyntax in TLA and a debate on crosslinguistic influence are introduced. In particular, the chapter compares the three most important models of language transfer advanced in the field of formal linguistics, i.e. the Cumulative Enhancement Model (CEM) (Flynn *et al.*, 2004), the Typological Primacy Model (TPM) (Rothman, 2011) and the Second Language (L2) Status Factor (L2SF) (Bardel & Falk, 2007). Additionally, it presents the most significant theories belonging to the holistic-catalytic approach, highlighting the fluidity of boundaries among the languages constituting the multilingual repertoire and the mutual influence among languages. The influence of the Dynamic System Theory (DST) will be analysed and discussed in terms of its implications on other theoretical approaches to multilingualism and in terms of the countability of languages (Herdina & Jessner, 2002; Hufeisen & Marx, 2007).

1.3 The Benefits of Language Learning and the Bilingual Paradox

Recent research shows that bilingualism can foster some aspects of cognitive abilities including metalinguistic skills and language learning abilities, understanding of other people's perspectives and mental flexibility in dealing with complex situations. For the learner, the acquisition of an L3 is aided by the knowledge of an L2 (Kroll, 2017; Petitto *et al.*, 2012). The literature is in broad agreement that L3 learners are at an advantage, be they learners that, as adults, add an L3 having acquired an L2 or children in multilingual societies who learn a foreign language in addition to their native language (typically a minority language) and the official language. The most consistent findings explain the advantages in terms of more developed awareness of the structure and functions of language itself, i.e. metalinguistic abilities (Adesope *et al.*, 2010; Grey *et al.*, 2018; Mohanty, 2019). More specifically, Rivers and Golonka (2009) summarise the advantages such learners enjoy in comparison to *ab initio* adult L2 learners as follows:

- the use of more metacognitive behaviours, particularly metacognitive self-management in the learning process used by the learner to direct the learner's in-class learning behaviours, as well as language use behaviours outside of the formal instructed environment;
- the use of a wider variety of cognitive learning strategies;
- more demonstration of autonomous learning;
- better affective behaviours and, in particular, a more positive attitude toward the learning process;
- higher proficiency outcomes for a given course length. (Rivers & Golonka, 2009: 259)

An extensive body of research suggests that the bilingual experience enhances executive control (e.g. Bialystok, 2020; Kroll & Bialystok, 2013). This may result in better performance on other complex cognitive tasks, including language learning, where ignoring non-relevant stimuli is required. Kroll and Bialystok (2013: 497) maintain that '[i]n the realm of cognitive processing, studies of executive function have demonstrated a bilingual advantage, with bilinguals outperforming their monolingual counterparts on tasks that require ignoring irrelevant information, tasks switching, and resolving conflict'.

Nonetheless, it must be argued that the interpretation of these findings has been questioned by a number of researchers who claim that these cognitive benefits are not always confirmed in the literature (e.g. Paap & Greenberg, 2013). It is not an easy task to find a unique explanation that accounts for both the advantages and disadvantages observed in bilinguals, in different cognitive domains. Bialystok (2009) suggests that the central conflict on the basis of bilingual language processing and production could explain the enhancement in executive control on the one hand and the slower lexical retrieval on the other. The latter compromises lexical access in that it is more effortful and enhances executive control through its continuous involvement in language production. In terms of memory, there is little impact; however, since memory performance relies on either linguistic or executive processing, monolinguals and bilinguals will perform differently depending on the type of task used.

To explain the so-called 'bilingual paradox', it can be argued that, first, bilingual language processing relies on a series of networks and, thus, it is not possible to identify one single cause to account for the different effects of bilingualism. Second, in regard to the research conducted before 1962, the negative effects reported were mainly due to sociopolitical reasons, i.e. discrimination towards immigrants and their bilingual children, and a weak and ineffective methodology where socioeconomic status, the type of bilingualism and the type of task employed were ignored or overlooked. Hence, the positive effects observed in a number of effective functions (EFs) such as inhibition, control, attentional networks, working memory (WM) and theory of mind (ToM), and the negative effects found in lexical retrieval, verbal fluency and vocabulary size can all be considered part of the complex, unique cognitive structure of bilingual language processing.

In addition, within the broader research on the cognitive effects of bilingualism, several studies have continued to support the notion of an existing threshold hypothesis for language learning. A study by Ardasheva and Tretter (2012) underlines that cognitive processing advantages associated with bilingual experiences may arise from children developing speaking proficiency in two languages receiving constant input. However, they observed that these cognitive processing benefits may result in higher academic performance only when the language of schooling is developed, particularly by means of literacy. Along similar lines, after a detailed review of works focused on the effects of bilingualism on EFs, cognitive aging and brain plasticity, Antoniou (2019: 408) claims that 'bilingual advantages are unlikely to extend to all bilinguals in all circumstances'. This observation accounts for some of the inconsistencies in the research findings on the cognitive effects of bilingualism. Specifically, the author explains them in terms of study design and different conceptualisations of bilingualism in research.

1.4 The Holistic Approach beyond Bilingual and Monolingual Systems

It can be claimed that any attempt to define the bilingual system as better or worse compared to the monolingual system would fail, in that, language deficit and control advantages constitute peculiar aspects of the bilingual mind, which makes it different from the monolingual mind. Accordingly, this chapter aims to describe the unique nature of bilinguals, together with their peculiar cognitive and linguistic system in language acquisition, not comparable to two (or more) monolinguals put together. The main reason is that bilingualism can be considered as a continuous dimension affected by a variety of linguistic, social and individual factors, rather than a dichotomous one. As mentioned, one of the main issues in the field of applied linguistics, particularly in bilingual education research, is that monolingualism has always been the default for human communication and additional language learning. Following this assumption, during the whole process of multilingual acquisition, language competence is always compared to an idealised monolingual native speaker instead of other multilinguals. More specifically, monolingual bias has been seen as a viewpoint that considers the prototypical human being as having only one language. It can be found in many subfields of research in linguistics, including second or additional language acquisition, psycholinguistics, neurolinguistics and language policy.

A number of negative consequences arise from taking for granted monolingualism as the perceived norm. The first and most evident issue related to the identification of the prototype is the difficulty in defining and distinguishing monolinguals, bilinguals and multilinguals. If the concept of monolingualism is rather explicit and understandable, the definition and features distinguishing bilinguals and multilinguals vary considerably based on a proficiency-level continuum going from the ability to communicate in more than one language to reaching native-like competence in multiple languages. It has been observed how monolingual bias is perpetuated in the two main fields of language acquisition, i.e. first language (L1) acquisition and SLA. 'Readers can find many books on each of these subjects, but there is only one chapter in any of these books devoted to bilingual acquisition, and multilingual acquisition is rarely mentioned' (Barratt, 2018: 2).

Due to the spread of the multilingual turn in applied linguistics, holistic perspectives have started to challenge all the traditional monolingual assumptions constituting the fundamental theoretical background of SLA research for decades. That is, researchers who conceptualise languages holistically are considered as innovative in that they openly question the traditional, widely acknowledged dichotomies of native/non-native speakers and the consequent view of the L2 learner as an incomplete or deficient speaker, the concept of ultimate attainment and fossilisation and the nature of L2 knowledge and processing (De Angelis, 2021). Holistic approaches to the study, testing and assessment of multilingual learners are characterised by the integration of multiple language resources taking into account language diversity and minority language-speaking practices. Moreover, the debate has contributed to a profound change in L2 research and has influenced the way scholars view and conceive languages, language boundaries and, most importantly, the impact of previously acquired languages in facilitating or hindering additional languages.

Indeed, it can be argued that the use of monolingualism as the prototype for humans clashes with the reality that bilinguals constitute the majority of the world's population. Grosjean (2014) points out that bilinguals and multilinguals outnumber monolinguals, and that bilingualism is found everywhere among all social classes and all ages. Even though the specific percentage of bilinguals cannot be verified due to the inability to define bilingualism univocally and the impossibility to count the world's languages accurately, it is estimated that more than half of the world's population is bilingual. More specifically, according to the *Ethnologue*, 'more than 7000 languages are spoken in 194 countries of the world, or approximately 38 languages per country' (as cited in Berthele, 2020: 10). Such a linguistic situation implies that the majority of the world's population lives with plurilingualism. Nonetheless, due to the aforementioned difficulty in defining bilingualism, providing an accurate estimate of the number of languages spoken in each country is simply not possible. The concept of bilingualism is fuzzy since the features defining what constitutes bilingualism make the boundaries blurry. What represents a prototypical bilingual has been seen to change according to particular cultural models of language competence in specific contexts. As Berthele observes, a prototypical bilingual is a balanced bilingual who uses two codes considered as 'proper' languages. Other dimensions considered in the portrait of bilingualism are age of onset, use of languages and attitudinal preferences.

In regard to stereotypes, Berthele (2020: 9) argues that, 'as opposed to birds, trees, and flowers, languages and dialects are not natural kinds'. They are emerging phenomena shaped by cognitive constraints and by the socioeconomic niche in which human communication takes place. Thus, considering that the nature of these phenomena is cultural, the categories and degrees of bilingualism are shaped by cultural ideas about languages and language users. Bilingualism is culturally different across the world. In addition, if one takes into account the different factors that contribute to characterising the phenomenon, including style, register, slang and other intra-language varieties, it can be argued that the whole world population can, in fact, be considered bilingual.

However, due to monolingual bias recognising native speaker competence as the benchmark, bilingual speakers are put in a position of disadvantage and inferiority since this approach focuses attention on what emergent bilinguals lack and the distance existing between them and the idealised monolingual speaker. To better understand the roots of the monolingual superior competence, it is worth recalling May's (2014: 35) quote: 'it is by virtue of from-birth exposure to, and primary socialisation into, only one language that the archetypical native speaker is imagined to possess a superior kind of linguistic competence, one whose purity proves itself in the absence of detectable traces of any other language during [...] language use'.

Therefore, emergent bilinguals or language learners 'permanently inhabit a place defined by incompleteness, inadequacy, and deficit' (Escobar, 2016: 250). In terms of research, the practice of reducing additional language learning to reaching a sort of monolingual-like competence has a number of negative implications which tend to marginalise the experience of additional language learning and use. In addition, the overemphasis on the monolingual standard and the consequent inability of bilinguals to conform to it has obscured the peculiarity of the process and the mechanism of additional language learning and has contributed to ignoring the multilingual repertoire with which bilinguals approach a third or additional language. The current work approaches the analysis of third or additional language acquisition from a more comprehensive point of view. That is, by going beyond the issue of why adult bilinguals do not reach the same level of proficiency as monolingual speakers.

To reach a better understanding of the new emerging picture, an interdisciplinary effort is required that redefines the standard of comparison in bilingualism research, which in turn has implications for the public understanding of bilingualism too. Research has shown that the L1 always changes in selective but predictable ways upon exposure to an L2 (Sorace, 2011, 2016). Not only do these findings reveal that language in the brain is highly adaptive but they also imply that bilinguals are not (and should not be expected to be) monolingual-like in either of their languages. Accordingly, the holistic approach propounded considers bilingual learners as unique individuals, with their peculiar linguistic and cognitive background, and considers the difference in becoming bilinguals later in life. In other words, instead of focusing on the proficiency level attained of the target language(s), it takes into account the whole linguistic repertoire and how the different languages interact among each other and contribute to multilingual competence during the process of language acquisition.

1.5 SLA vs TLA: Cognitive and Linguistic Differences

As already mentioned, after nearly three decades of intense research on TLA, it is now commonly agreed that there are several cognitive and linguistic reasons to consider TLA as an independent field of study from SLA (Aronin & Hufeisen, 2009). Until very recently, L3 learners were included under the umbrella of learners of an L2. However, it has been argued (González-Alonso et al., 2016) that L2 and L3 learners come to the process of language acquisition with a linguistic and cognitive background that differs considerably, both quantitatively and qualitatively. Indeed, an L2 learner is a monolingual at the initial stage of SLA, whereas an L3 learner is already a bilingual (potentially early/late, simultaneous/consecutive, etc.). This entails that having at least two languages in their linguistic repertoires allows L3 learners to relate new structures, new vocabulary or new ways of expressing communicative functions to the two languages they already know, not just one of them, as in the case of monolinguals. Moreover, L3 learners show more refined skills and strategies for achieving the language learning task due to the transfer of language learning and training.

Another striking difference between the two processes concerns the learning context. SLA usually means that the L2 is chronologically learned after the L1. However, the differences between SLA and TLA not only refer to the order of acquisition of the languages involved but also concern the method of acquisition since the L2/Ln can be learned in a variety of different ways. For example, it can be studied as a foreign language for a few hours a week at school, or it may be the language of instruction or the main language of the community. What is more, the differences could also relate to the many other factors involved in the complex area of research on TLA, i.e. age, instructional methods or motivation. Most importantly, in TLA, all these differences must be considered not only for the target language but also for the L2 mastered by the learner. TLA is a very common process among early bilinguals who have acquired their two first languages simultaneously. A further difference related to the learning context concerns language use. That is, some L3 learners are active bilinguals who use their other two languages in their everyday life, while others live in a monolingual context and use their L2, in this case, a foreign language, only occasionally.

Additionally, in terms of the order of acquisition of the languages, the two processes of language acquisition differ considerably. There are only two possible routes in SLA, i.e. the two languages are either learned simultaneously or one after the other. In TLA, instead, the number of possible routes increases as there are at least four main types of order of acquisition (Cenoz, 2001). The three languages can be acquired consecutively (L1 > L2 > L3); two languages can be acquired simultaneously before the L3 is acquired (Lx/Ly > L3); or after the first languages (L1 > Lx/Ly); or the three languages could be acquired simultaneously in early trilingualism (Lx/Ly/Lz). Finally, among the other factors affecting the process of TLA, it is worth mentioning the status of the different languages involved, the degree of bilingualism and the type of bilingualism in the L1 and L2 (or Lx and Ly) presented by the learners when acquiring the L3. More specifically, the study of attitudes towards the different languages included in the multilingual repertoire has yielded results linked to individual factors such as age and dominant home language (Sagasta Errasti, 2003), and language status and sociobiographical factors (Rothman & Guijarro-Fuentes, 2012).

Thus, with TLA, a new holistic approach to research is advanced to challenge the discussed monolingual bias in research on multilinguals. This requires a new methodology which takes into account three main aspects, i.e. the multilingual speaker, the whole linguistic repertoire of the language learners and the context of acquisition. Regarding the first aspect, as Grosjean (1992) and Cook (2003) point out, multilingual speakers cannot be considered as several monolinguals of different languages put together as their multilingual competence is of a different type. Indeed, Kecskes (2010: 100) claims that these differences are not only quantitative but also qualitative in that 'monolingual and bilingual children do not differ in what they do with languages, but in how they do it'. Specifically, according to the author, there are conceptual differences between monolinguals and bilinguals. For instance, bilinguals use strategies such as code-switching and translanguaging in additional language learning that are not used by monolinguals when dealing with an L2 (García, 2008). Code-switching, in particular, has been considered as the most distinctive feature of bilingual speakers. Therefore, it is important to be aware of the fact that, in studies on the effects of bilingualism on TLA, comparisons between monolinguals and bilinguals must be considered carefully in that two different types of competencies are being compared.

Another important issue deserving attention is the difference between two types of L3 learners: active bilinguals and so-called foreign language users. Psycholinguistic studies on TLA have usually compared active bilinguals to monolinguals, highlighting the benefits of bilingualism on cognitive and enhanced metalinguistic awareness (MLA). However, the focus on a multilingualism approach suggests looking at the different types of L3 learners to see whether the cognitive benefits can be extended to those learners who have just acquired a foreign language but do not use it regularly in a multilingual context. In other words, if the advantages of bilingualism in TLA are mainly due to the constant use of previous languages or to other factors such as the level of bilingualism achieved or the age of acquisition of the L2. Therefore, considering different types of L3 learners means attending to how bilingual speakers integrate an L3 into their linguistic repertoire and the fluidity between their three languages.

The second aspect taken into account in TLA is the focus on the whole linguistic repertoire instead of 'one language only' or 'one language at a time'. Indeed, to consider the complexity of multilingualism and how the different subsystems are connected across the languages in their development, it is necessary to look at all the languages in the multilingual speaker's repertoire. As will be explained in more detail in the following sections, the DST of SLA can be used to interpret the effects of bilingualism on TLA. In fact, by looking at the interaction among languages in the multilingual learner's repertoire, it is possible to identify 'connected growers' that facilitate TLA. The expression 'connected growers' was first used by De Bot *et al.* (2007) to refer to the aforementioned DST. However, as Cenoz (2013) notes, it can be useful to explain the interaction between different languages particularly when the scores obtained in the three languages mastered are correlated and the patterns of crosslinguistic interaction are analysed. In other words, additional language learners apply the grammatical and pragmatic elements of their L1 and L2 to better understand and infer the mechanisms of the third or additional target language.

Finally, the third component to be considered in the focus on a multilingualism approach is the context of use of each language, as multilinguals build up their competence in social interaction. Indeed, the importance of context when analysing the effects of bilingualism on TLA aims at explaining how the L3 is incorporated into the multilingual speaker's language practices. To sum up, the alternative approach of focus on multilingualism proposes to study the influence of bilingualism on TLA based on the whole linguistic repertoire and the interaction between language repertoires. At the same time, it considers the acquisition and use of languages in relation to the social context (De Angelis, 2007).

Another interesting approach looking at multilingualism from a multicompetence perspective comes from the dominant language constellation (DLC) propounded by Aronin. She explains it in the following terms: 'the group of the most important languages for a particular individual, enabling as a whole unit, the person to act in a multilingual environment and to meet all his/her needs' (Aronin, 2006: 145). The relationship between the languages of multicompetence in the individual and in the community is portrayed as a constellation of inner circle languages, orbited by the languages of the linguistic repertoire. More specifically, the number of languages in a DLC is about three, with others coming into play in particular circumstances.

1.6 Monolingual, Bilingual and Multilingual Speech Production Models

One of the most significant differences between SLA and TLA is the cognitive profile of the learners. That is to say, monolinguals and bilinguals have been seen to process linguistic information differently. The following section provides a comprehensive account of the most important speech production models currently available in the psycholinguistic literature. Since most of the models of multilingual speech production are based on models originally created for monolingual speakers, it is worth starting with an overview of monolingual and bilingual speech production models. The aim is to highlight the main features of each model and how they influenced the development of multilingual speech production models.

1.6.1 Levelt's speaking model

Levelt's (1989) influential 'speaking' model, developed for monolingual processing, was used by De Bot (1992) and Clyne (2003) as a basis for their reflections on multilingual production. Levelt states that speech processing takes place in successive steps in three information stores, i.e. the conceptualiser, the formulator and the articulator. The conceptualiser transforms communicative intuitions into preverbal messages.

It allows the speaker to access extra-linguistic world knowledge as well as the individual communicative situation. Messages are received by the formulator, which has access to the lexicon.

The formulator converts the preverbal message into meaning. Conversion occurs through the activation of semantic, syntactic, morphological and phonological information at the lemma and lexeme levels. Precisely, the lemma part contains the word's semantic and syntactic information, whereas the lexeme part specifies the possible forms of the word. Lemma activation is argued to be the first to take place. Once the output of the formulator (i.e. phonetic plan) is ready, it passes on to the articulator to be converted into overt speech. The phonetic plan (i.e. internal speech) is further checked via the speech comprehension system so that any errors can be detected and rectified before the overt speech is produced.

1.6.2 De Bot's bilingual production model

De Bot (1992) uses Levelt's model as the basis for his reflections on multilingual production. Indeed, as already mentioned, all models of multilingual speech production are essentially extended or revised models of monolingual and bilingual speech production models. In fact, as De Angelis (2007) observes, it would be more accurate to state that no models are specifically formulated to account for multilingual speech production. Instead, only models of monolingual and bilingual speech production account for multilingual production as well. In particular, De Bot's model accounts for the speech of healthy individuals and is not specifically concerned with language disorders, language learning processes or language skills other than speaking. The author emphasises that Levelt's model is particularly reliable as it is based on 'several decades of psycholinguistic research and is based on a wealth of empirical data, obtained through experimental research and the observation of speech errors' (De Bot, 1992: 2). Therefore, he claims that the bilingual version of the model only needs some minor modifications to be adapted to work efficiently.

In addition, it is crucial to note that the model was also extended to multilingual speech production. This means that one of the most comprehensive and detailed proposals of multilingual speech production available in the literature today is based on a framework empirically based on monolingual data. However, according to De Bot (2004), our knowledge of how languages interact in the multilingual mind is still too limited to make a specific model for multilingual processing necessary. In his bilingual model, De Bot describes how selection and control work in a bilingual speaker. Accordingly, he also draws on Green's inhibition/activation model. De Bot introduces a language mode with a monitoring function. It provides information about the state of activation of various languages and acts as a monitoring device which compares the intended language with the language currently used. According to the author, the main conditions that a bilingual speech production model should satisfy are:

(1) to account for the speaker's ability to use languages separately or mix them during speech, as is the case with code-switching;
(2) to account for instances of crosslinguistic influence;
(3) it should not be concerned with the speed of production as the use of several languages should not slow down the entire production process;
(4) it should be able to account for the different levels of proficiency of the bilingual's languages;
(5) it should be able to cope with a potentially unlimited number of languages and must be able to represent interactions between these different languages.

In order to satisfy these requirements and apply them to multiple languages, a number of changes to Levelt's original model were necessary. First of all, referring to the conceptualiser, De Bot's rationale is built upon two main considerations, i.e. Levelt's discussion on registers and the knowledge of how concepts are lexicalised in different languages. De Bot agrees with Levelt's principle that information on language registers is added to the preverbal message in the conceptualiser and extends it to the bilingual version. Regarding the second point, De Bot additionally takes into account the difference in the way concepts are lexicalised in different languages and argues that language-specific information must necessarily be added to the preverbal message in the conceptualiser.

In terms of the formulator, he first proposes two scenarios which see, respectively, the existence of one common lexicon for both languages where information is distinguished through a labelling system and, on the other hand, two separate formulators and lexicons for each language involved. In a second phase, the author advances a solution that is somehow in the middle of the two extremes proposed earlier. That is, some elements of the two languages are stored together and some others are stored separately, depending on variables such as linguistic distance and proficiency level. Finally, regarding the articulator phase of the model, Levelt maintains that speakers store a large number of syllables rather than sounds.

The phonetic plan is argued to consist of strings of such syllables. De Bot (2004) proposes that bilinguals have a common store for the syllables of both languages, and patterns are stored only once if they are identical in the two languages, or individually if there are no matching patterns. The idea that syllables belonging to different languages are all grouped in a common store raised a number of questions. It was argued that some language-specific labelling mechanism was required, otherwise the learner would not be able to match incoming information with the syllables. De Bot clarifies this point by stating that speakers have all sounds and patterns in the mind. However, it is still not clear how these sounds are distinguished during the production process. He maintains that learners initially apply the L1 norms to L2 sounds and then, once L2 proficiency reaches a level that allows the two systems to become independent, they no longer need to rely on the L1. This mechanism would also account for the crosslinguistic phenomena attested from L1 to L2.

1.6.3 Green

The model proposed by Green (1986, 1998) is particularly relevant for the purpose of the current discussion as it has been used as a starting point by a number of authors, including De Bot, to develop their own speech production model. From his studies on code-switching and bilingual aphasia, Green concluded that bilingual speakers do not switch their languages on and off, rather, their languages show different levels of activation. Specifically, in order to explain how control is executed, Green combines the notion of activation and inhibition, suggesting that they operate concurrently during the production process. When an item from the target language is selected, the activation of the item itself occurs together with the inhibition of all its competitors from other non-target languages.

When inhibition occurs, the activation level of all potential competitors is raised, reducing the possibility that the incorrect item will be selected in place of the target item. Accordingly, the highest level of activation occurs when a language is selected and controls the output. In a speech situation, all the languages available to the bilingual speaker are then selected to varying degrees. For instance, a language may be selected as the language to speak, being active as it takes part in the speech processor, or dormant as it is stored in the long-term memory but not interacting in the speech process. The speakers control the activation and inhibition process by using a number of resources, constantly replenished by a resource generator. Resources have been compared to the energy of the production system. However, there are situations in which the speaker will not have full access to the resources. For instance, when they are not completely focused as only a limited amount of energy can be used at a given time. In the case of L2 speakers and learners, the amount of energy required is clearly larger as their L2 system is not as automatised as their L1 system. When the speaker has insufficient resources to use, types of 'errors blends' described by Green (e.g. strying, springling) can occur in production.

The underlying theoretical argument to Green's model is that the way aphasic patients behave indicates a problem associated with the control of 'intact language systems'. He maintains that languages cannot be lost after injuries. They simply become less accessible during comprehension and production. Therefore, the aforementioned errors found in the speech of healthy individuals reflect poor control of the intact system. Although this latter has not been explicitly defined by the author, from what he writes, it has been inferred (De Angelis, 2007) that an intact system is a system containing native-like knowledge. Assuming that language knowledge is native-like allows the analysis of speech production without being concerned with defining the type of knowledge in the mind. Consequently, from this point of view, any language in the mind represents an intact system, entailing that it can be added without the need to define its content. Following these principles, the model has also been extended to multilingual speakers.

One of the main questions raised was the extent to which multiple languages could effectively be controlled in the multilingual mind. As already mentioned, Green argues that languages can be activated to varying degrees and are presented in one of the following states: selected (i.e. controlling speech output), active (i.e. playing a role in ongoing processing) or dormant (i.e. residing in long-term memory but exerting no effects on ongoing processing). It is the frequency of use of each language that determines in which of the three states it resides. For example, the language used more frequently can remain active in the background during online processing and the parallel activity that occurs results in a sort of influence on the target language. Instead, languages that are not used for a long time are in a dormant state and do not affect online processing. In addition, about 10 years later, Green (1998) developed the inhibitory model emphasising multiple levels of control. In particular, a language task inhibits potential competitors from production at the lemma level resorting to language tags. A supervisory attentional system monitors the established scheme. The switching cost is defined as asymmetrical in that switching to the suppressed language, in unbalanced bilinguals, takes longer.

1.7 Formal Approaches to Multilingual Acquisition: Crosslinguistic Influence in Third Language Acquisition

Formal approaches to multilingual language acquisition have been put forward in the last two decades to answer the main question of which patterns of previously acquired languages (i.e. L1 or L2) are likely to be transferred, and to what extent, to a third or additional language. As Rothman (2015: 181) points out, studying multilingual acquisition 'permits a unique window into language and cognition in ways that cannot be seen in monolingualism or bilingualism'. Scholars particularly focus on whether there is wholesale transfer of structural properties or lexical items of a source language or specific features from each language (see González-Alonso *et al.*, 2016).

Despite the different theoretical backgrounds assumed as a starting point by researchers, they all share the main focus of investigation, which is how the linguistic parser solves the optionality coming from the unique L3 setting, as two or more systems are potentially available to influence the acquisition of the target L3. Moreover, a number of commonly shared assumptions can be identified within the formal approach area of research. First, all the languages constituting the multilingual repertoire are identifiable entities that can be labelled following the point of view of chronological acquisition, i.e. L1, L2, L3, etc. Second, multilingual speakers' languages are categorical identities and a comparison of the morphosyntactic structures used is a criterion to make inferences on crosslinguistic influence. The final assumption is that the initial stage of TLA can be investigated and it is possible to detect crosslinguistic influences from the different languages which can be a potential source of transfer (Berthele, 2020: 12).

To examine the mechanisms that regulate the L3/Ln crosslinguistic influence, the majority of scholars dealing with TLA in the last decade mainly focused on lexicon, lexical access and retrieval (Cenoz, 2003). It was commonly agreed that crosslinguistic influence and transfer come from either the L1 or L2; however, a number of other factors remained unexplored such as the role of dialects and varieties as potentially relevant categories in the repertoire. In particular, in TLA, the main issues concern the languages with the most prominent role involved and the reason for this predominance. A number of factors from formal approaches to the L3 morphosyntax were considered such as proficiency, activation, L2 status and typological similarity between the L3 and the previously learned languages. It has been claimed (González-Alonso & Rothman, 2017) that the greater complexity of L3/Ln learning is due to two main aspects. The first concerns the initial stages of interlanguage formation, in that multiple grammatical configurations are present in the learner's mind and all are available for transfer. The second aspect deals with the lower predictability of developmental patterns, both linguistically and non-linguistically, that are supposed to be affected by crosslinguistic influence and a number of other cognitive factors. As is the case for all initial stages of language learning irrespective of age and experience, L3 learners are faced with a large amount of input. On the one hand, the L3 situation is similar to SLA for the previous linguistic experience to draw from as a source of transfer; however, on the other hand, the L3/Ln setting is unique in that the learner's previous linguistic experience is not limited to one language.

Importantly, all models advanced assume that the transfer does not happen randomly and that one or more linguistic and cognitive factors take precedence over others in determining which of the previously acquired languages are selected as a source of transfer. The morphosyntactic models of transfer in an L3, selected and reviewed in this chapter, are the CEM (Flynn *et al.*, 2004), the L2SF Model (Falk & Bardel, 2010, 2011) and the TPM (Rothman, 2011). As will be discussed in the following sections, they mainly vary along a temporal or quantitative dimension in terms of how they conceptualise transfer in TLA. In other words, the models either focus on the point at which the language transfer of the predominant language occurs or on the wholesale versus property-specific transfer. In addition, another feature shared by all the models considered is the underlying assumption that transfer takes place as a result of cognitive economy, in order to avoid redundancy in language acquisition.

1.7.1 Cumulative Enhancement Model

The CEM, developed by Flynn *et al.* (2004), claims that transfer takes place on a property-by-property basis through development. It represents both a model of the initial stage as well as a theory of developmental and attainment in an L3. The CEM has been considered as the first L3/Ln initial stage model, despite some previous linguistic works on L3 syntax (e.g. Klein, 1995). The authors maintain that transfer at the initial stage and beyond is supposed to be maximally facilitative. Indeed, they argue that developmental patterns are not redundant and that language acquisition is facilitated since each prior language can either enhance TLA or remain neutral. They insist that previous linguistic knowledge is expected to transfer in multilingual development only when a positive effect is observed. Otherwise, the transfer does not take place.

In brief, the model entails that the learning process is cumulative and that all the languages that the learner is familiar with can potentially affect (i.e. enhance) the development of the target language. Therefore, the privileged role of the L1 as a source of transfer is no longer supported, in that all the languages involved in the multilingual system play a significant role in additional language acquisition. The authors advance this proposal in a series of studies on relative clauses on adults and children and the consequent comparison of the results for L1, L2 and L3 acquisition. Specifically, for TLA, they tested three types of relative clauses:

(1) lexical head with semantic content (e.g. 'the owner questioned the businessman who greeted the worker');
(2) lexical head with no semantic content (e.g. 'the janitor criticised the person who called the lawyer');
(3) free relative (e.g. 'the professor introduced whoever greeted').

The major strength of this research design has been considered to be the choice of the languages used for the experiment, very different from a morphosyntactic point of view (De Angelis, 2007). Indeed, the participants' L1 is Kazakh, i.e. a Turkish language with a head-final, left-branching structure like Japanese. On the other hand, Russian, the participants' L2, is a Slavic language with a head-initial, right-branching structure like English. Therefore, if in the acquisition of English L3, learners rely on their prior knowledge regarding the relative clause structure in English, evidence of the use of a right-branching language would suggest an influence of the Russian L2. This latter, in turn, would provide evidence for the CEM of acquisition. Thus, by demonstrating that previously learned grammars are used as a source to rely upon during additional language acquisition, Flynn et al. (2004) provide a valuable contribution to the field of research for a number of reasons. First, they show that previous non-native languages can influence the attainment of an L3/Ln to a significant extent, even when proficiency in the L2 is low or intermediate. Second, the influence of the order of acquisition is also highlighted as, in the study, the possible difference between simultaneous and sequential acquisition was also taken into account.

1.7.2 L2 Status Factor Model

The L2SF Model does not support a strong position regarding the aforementioned argument about wholesale versus property-by-property transfer. Instead, it maintains that the largest amount of default L2 transfer would come at the earliest stages. On the privileged role taken by the L2 in the initial stage of L3 syntax, it has been argued that the L2 acts as a filter to the L1 grammar. To advance this hypothesis, Bardel and Falk examined two different groups of participants, i.e. L1 verb second (V2)/L2 non-V2 on the one hand, and L1 non-V2/L2 V2 on the other, both learning Swedish or Dutch as an L3. The results of the experiment demonstrated that the L2 Dutch/German group, who did not have a V2 L1, performed better than the L2 English group, whose L1 was V2, in producing post-verbal negation. The authors argue that only a privileged role for the L2 could account for these findings.

The L2SF is a particularly strong hypothesis since it allows us to make valuable predictions that are testable independently of the language pairings. In other words, the authors suggested that the L2SF determined the transfer source, independently of the relative typological similarity or genetic relatedness of the languages involved. According to Falk and Bardel (2010, 2011), the L2SF is an outcome of the higher degree of cognitive similarity between an L2 and L3 than between an L1 and L3. In addition, L2 and L3 learning have a number of other features in common. In Falk and Bardel (2010, 2011), it was suggested that the L2SF is an outcome of the higher degree of similarity between an L2 and L3 than between an L1 and L3, regarding age of onset, outcome, learning situation, degree of metalinguistic knowledge, learning strategies and degree of awareness in the process of language appropriation. Hence, the differences just mentioned between the acquisition of an L1 and the learning of an L2 and an L3 might, in fact, account for why the L2 is often present and sometimes even preferred over the L1 as a transfer source.

An interesting approach comes from the neurolinguistic framework which supports Falk and Bardel's model (2011), that is the declarative/procedural memory elaborated by Paradis (1994). Indeed, the declarative and procedural memory systems are well studied and constitute a powerful basis for predictions about language acquisition within a neurolinguistic approach. Paradis (1994) was first to point out the fundamental difference between procedural and declarative memory in relation to implicit linguistic competence and explicit metalinguistic knowledge, respectively. Specifically, he claims:

> Within the framework of the implicit/explicit perspective [...], all late-learned languages (L2, L3, Ln) are sustained to a large extent by declarative memory. As such, they are more likely to manifest dynamic interference from one another than from the native language(s). (Paradis, 2008: 344)

Following Paradis' view, in an L1, procedural memory sustains the implicit linguistic structure (i.e. phonology, morphology, syntax and lexicon) whereas the declarative memory sustains vocabulary (i.e. words as form-meaning pairs). While L1 grammar is implicitly acquired and sustained by procedural memory, L2 grammar ('to the extent that teaching of L2 is formal') is based on explicit knowledge and sustained by declarative memory. Therefore, since vocabulary is sustained by declarative memory in an L2 as well as in an L1, there is a more obvious difference between an L1 and an L2 (Ln) when it comes to phonology, morphology, syntax and the morphosyntactic properties of the lexicon. Indeed, these latter components are acquired implicitly in an L1 while they are learned explicitly in an L2/Ln.

1.7.3 Typological Proximity Model

Different from the model advanced by Bardel and Falk discussed above, another influential model put forward by Rothman (2011), the TPM, proposes multiple sources of transfer in multilingual syntactic acquisition. It explicates a hypothesised instance of initial stages wholesale transfer of one of the previously acquired languages, the result of which is assumed as the initial interlanguage grammar of the L3. The TPM has also been considered as a more restricted version of the CEM (Flynn *et al.*, 2004), reviewed in this chapter, in that neither of the models predicts absolute, categorical transfer from an L1 or an L2. On the other hand, if the CEM claims that multilingual language learning is determined by the cumulative effect of previous linguistic acquisition, the TPM assumes that transfer is conditioned by factors related to the psychotypology aspects between the languages involved.

Besides, what differentiates the two models is the assumption of the TPM that transfer is constrained by either typological proximity or perceived proximity between the three grammars. That is, the typologically closest language to the L3 between the L1 and L2 has priority to be selected as a source of transfer, even when the transfer is not facilitative and causes errors in the production of the L3. In this particular case, typological proximity refers to psychotypology, i.e. the perceived similarity or language distance as suggested by Kellerman (1983). Importantly, the TPM assumes that learners already have some sort of awareness of language typology as well as of typological proximity between two languages. However, it is not clearly explained to what extent learners must be consciously aware of these factors. In the case of equally distant or equally close languages, the model makes no predictions.

It has been argued (Rothman & Guijarro-Fuentes, 2012) that since all the models advance different assumptions regarding non-facilitative transfer, it is possible to test them against one another under the right conditions. In particular, Rothman (2010) tested them by examining the L3 acquisition of Brazilian Portuguese, comparing two groups of L3 learners, i.e. L1 speakers of English who were highly successful Spanish learners and L1 speakers of Spanish who were highly successful learners of L2 English. The experiment was focused on word order restrictions and relative clause attachment preference. The choice of languages is particularly relevant since if it is true that Spanish and Brazilian Portuguese are typologically similar, in fact, Brazilian Portuguese patterns are more similar to English regarding the features under investigation. The findings demonstrate that Spanish was preferred as a source of transfer independently of the order of acquisition and despite the fact that English would have been a more facilitative option. Therefore, on the basis of these observations, Rothman maintained that the results provide evidence in favour of the TPM and against the predictions of the CEM as well as those of the L2SF. Moreover, the author found similar effects when investigating the area of adjective placement and semantic entailments (Rothman, 2011).

All three models examined and discussed in this chapter, i.e. CEM, TPM and L2SF, despite proposing different views in terms of the impact of L1 and L2 on L3 learning, make similar predictions regarding the role of typological proximity. Specifically, they all agree that prior L2 learning experience with a typologically similar L2 will enhance L3 learning more than experience with a typologically different L2. However, it has been argued (Park & Starr, 2014) that all these models are based on data drawn from late bilinguals. That is to say, they acquired their L1 in infancy and only later studied an L2. Therefore, in their study, they examine whether the models also apply to early bilinguals. In contrast to Rothman's results, Park and Starr (2014) did not find a significant effect of L2 typological proximity when learning an L3 among early bilinguals.

Moreover, the study provides additional evidence to support the view that any language learning experience, in a formal setting, is advantageous in learning additional languages. Accordingly, the data indicate that the transfer of previous language knowledge does not represent the underlying mechanism which accounts for the benefits of bilingualism in TLA. Instead, it appears that the advantage may come from the general level of MLA developed through learning languages in a formal setting.

1.8 Grosjean's Language Mode Hypothesis

Grosjean's bilingual view has been most influential in research on multilingualism for a number of reasons. He maintains that the speech of bilinguals and multilinguals is regulated by different modes in which the speaker can be set during speaking. Specifically, he explains the Language Mode Hypothesis in these terms:

> A mode is a state of activation of the bilinguals' language and language processing mechanisms. This state is controlled by such variables as who the bilingual is speaking or listening to, the situation, the topic, the purpose of the interaction, and so on. (Grosjean, 1998: 136)

The author argues that, on one end of the continuum, bilinguals are in a totally monolingual language mode when they interact or listen to monolinguals who only know one of the languages they master. On the other end of the continuum, bilinguals are in a bilingual language mode, that is, when they are interacting or listening to bilinguals who share two or more of the languages they speak. In the first case, one language is active in the mind and the other is deactivated. In the second case, both languages are active but the one that is used as the main language of processing is more active than the other(s). In between the two endpoints described, bilinguals also find themselves at intermediary points, depending on the influence of the factors named by Grosjean.

Indeed, he also defines the language mode as a 'state of activation of the bilingual's languages and language processing mechanism at a certain point in time' (Grosjean, 2001: 2). Among the factors named by the author, it is worth mentioning the participants' language mixing habits, the usual mode of interaction, the presence of monolinguals, the degree of formality and the form and content of the message. Grosjean's Language Mode Hypothesis is particularly suitable to apply to speakers of several languages, as languages can be activated to varying degrees during the speaking process and influence the target language output. Nonetheless, its validity still needs to be assessed more systematically with multilingual speakers. An interesting attempt comes from the study by Dewaele (2001). He looked at the interaction between three languages, Dutch, English and French, on the language mode continuum using a corpus of French interlanguage produced by 25 adult participants, in an informal and a formal context. The main findings revealed that the formality of the situation was a determining factor identifying the position of the speaker on the language mode continuum. Moreover, code-switches were less numerous in the formal situation, suggesting a general move towards the monolingual end of the continuum. Interestingly, the 'frequency of communication in French' had a greater impact on the interlanguage than the status of the interlanguage (L2 versus L3, i.e. the amount and the length of formal instruction in French).

1.9 The Factor Model: L3/Ln Acquisition in Instructed Contexts

Hufeisen's model has been developed to explain the foreign language process with a special focus on multiple acquisition in an instructed context. It takes into account the factors that influence the language acquisition process. Specifically, Hufeisen (1998) describes four initial stages of language acquisition, referring to the four languages that the learner is acquiring. As reported by Jessner (2008a), for each stage, the factors affecting the language learning process are as follows:

(a) neurophysiological factors which provide both the basis for and the precondition of general language learning, production and reception capability;
(b) learner external factors such as sociocultural and socioeconomic surroundings, including culture-specific learning traditions, type and amount of input the learner is exposed to;
(c) emotional factors such as anxiety, motivation or acceptance of the new target language;
(d) cognitive factors such as language awareness, linguistic and meta-linguistic awareness, learning awareness, knowledge of one's own learner type and the ability to employ learning strategies and techniques;
(e) linguistic factors as included in the learner's L1(s).

These factors have been reported to exclusively affect and characterise L3 learners. They explain why TLA has a catalytic effect, unique to multilingual learners, that contributes to distinguishing it from the field of SLA. More specifically, commenting on Hufeisen's model, Jessner points out that (the aforementioned factors):

> Explain why TLA cannot be subsumed under SLA [...]. Whereas the L2 learner is a complete beginner in the learning process of a second or first foreign language, the L3 learner already knows about the foreign language learning process and has [...] gathered individual techniques and strategies to deal with such a situation with differing degrees of success.

Additionally, the learner may have intuitively learned about her/his individual learner style. (Jessner, 2008a: 23)

Thus, Hufeisen's model is particularly relevant for the purpose of the current discussion in that it focuses on the reasons that make SLA and TLA two different processes that need to be examined separately. She addresses the issue by advancing a number of convincing arguments explaining why TLA cannot be subsumed under the umbrella of SLA. First of all, while the L2 learner is a complete beginner in the learning process of a second or first foreign language, the L3 learner is already familiar with the foreign language learning process. Accordingly, they have already developed a number of individual techniques and strategies to learn a new language. In addition, learners may have already learned to be aware of their individual learning style. Hufeisen illustrates the prototypical language learning process by taking into account each individual learning situation for the analysis. According to the author, each learner will develop a specific factor complex, where some factors turn out to be particularly predominant for the learners while some others do not exert a significant influence on the learning situation. All these new features involved belong to a new set of factors, i.e. foreign/L2-specific factors (such as the individual L2 learning experience), explicit or implicit foreign language learning strategies and interlanguages of other learned languages. It has been argued that it is at this stage that the L2 works as a supporting language in the TLA process. That is to say, L3 learners have language-specific knowledge and competencies at their disposal that L2 learners do not.

1.10 The Multilingual Processing Model

The Multilingual Processing Model, developed by Meißner (2004), accounts for the processes taking place during the reception phase of written and oral texts in a foreign language. Ideally, the language belongs to a typologically related family, following the assumption that the learner will develop receptive skills in all the languages related to the one that they already know. Hence, the focus is on the underlying processes that facilitate and enable the understanding of a new language. The basic assumption of the model is the idea that learners constantly rely on the knowledge they have in previous languages to understand a new text in the unknown language. Where two typologically related languages are involved, the hypotheses are constantly revised by the learner. This process has been seen as a spontaneous 'hypothetical grammar', relying more on the system of the previously learned languages than on the target one. During the learning process, the spontaneous grammar is constantly revised by the learner and developed by adding the structure and lexicon of the target language. As the structure of the previously known language is close to the target language, they work as a sort of matrix for the structures and lexicon to be compared and contrasted.

A number of preconditions must be met for spontaneous grammar to occur:

(a) an etymological relationship between the languages should exist;
(b) the learner has to be proficient in the bridge language(s);
(c) the learner has to be instructed on how to use the knowledge of a previously learned language as a bridge language.

When all the aforementioned conditions are met, the development of receptive skills goes through four different stages. The initial understanding of the first stage is facilitated by the bridge language. In particular, the generation and revision of the hypotheses for this grammar about interlingual regularities work in a dynamic way, by systemising and generalising the target language input.

At the second stage, through spontaneous grammar, an interlingual correspondence grammar is created, which constructs interlingual correspondence rules. An evident feature of this interlingual correspondence grammar can be seen in the transfer between the source and target languages. The third stage consists of a multilingual intersystem where all the interlingual transfer processes are stored. Thanks to this transfer base, the learner is provided with a general framework for decoding and understanding the new language. Among the most important transfer bases, it is worth mentioning the communicative strategy transfer, the transfer of interlingual processing procedures and the transfer of cognitive principles. The final stage stores all the learning experiences in the target language as metacognitive strategies. Over time, the learner develops the ability to construct multilingual system knowledge based on positive and negative correspondence rules.

1.11 The Dynamic Model of Multilingualism

The research on TLA has been particularly influenced by the already discussed model of bilingual processing, advanced by Grosjean. What is relevant about this latter model is the fact that it presents the bilingual learner as multicompetent, with specific speaking and processing abilities that make the bilingual learner not comparable to the monolingual in either language. This holistic approach to the linguistic system was also adopted by Herdina and Jessner's (2002) model, with a specific focus on the dynamics of multilingualism. This holistic-catalytic approach is more oriented towards proficiency in the sense of the skills-oriented tradition in applied linguistics and bilingualism research. The changing nature of multilingual development required scholars to restructure their ways of thinking about it. Indeed, they applied the DST, also known as complexity theory, taken from the fields of mathematics, physics and biology, to the study of multilingualism. The DST maintains that the subsystems of a complex system need to be considered as a whole in the way they affect overall and individual development.

Herdina and Jessner's Dynamic Model of Multilingualism (DMM) claims that the development of a multilingual system is characterised by changeability, non-linearity, reversibility (e.g. it may result in language attrition and loss), complexity, maintenance, interdependence and change of quality. In addition, it is also highly variable because it depends on social, psycholinguistic and individual factors. Hence, the model is designed as an autonomous model that is able to bridge the discussed gap between the research on the effects of bilingualism and the research on TLA. It suggests that future language acquisition studies should go beyond the study of language contact between two languages in order to include other types of bilingualism, considered as the knowledge of two or multiple languages. Moreover, it allows predicting multilingual development based on the factors involved in the process.

More specifically, the starting point of the DMM is the existence of a number of psycholinguistic systems (i.e. LS1/LS2/LS3, etc.), defined as open systems, which depend on psychological factors. Each system is interdependent and not autonomous from the other systems but, rather, perceived in mainstream research. Herdina and Jessner (2002: 150) claim that the language subsystems 'interact with each other and influence each other within the complex and dynamic system we call multilingualism'. In the DMM, the stability of the system depends on language maintenance. The language choices of multilingual speakers are affected by the perceived communicative needs. Therefore, the holistic approach described in the model is crucial to understand the dynamic interaction among complex systems in multilingual language processing. Accordingly, multilingual proficiency (MP) is described as the dynamic interaction among various psycholinguistic systems, crosslinguistic interaction (CLIN) and the M(ultilingualism)-factor or M-effect (see Jessner, 2008b): LS1, LS2, LS3, LSN + M-factor = MP.

The M-factor refers to all the features of multilingual systems that distinguish a bi/multilingual from a monolingual. That is to say, all the qualities developed in multilingual learners and speakers which cannot be described and observed in a cumulative way. MLA, for instance, represents one of these qualities, as a result of the increase in language contacts by multilinguals. The Multilingualism-factor is regarded as one of the most important properties that contributes to the enhancement of bilinguals' performance in a third or additional language. As will be discussed in more detail in Chapter 3, the key variable responsible for their improved outcome in TLA is the level of MLA. It consists of a set of skills or abilities developed by multilingual learners as a result of their prior linguistic and metacognitive knowledge. In particular, the catalytic effect of TLA has mainly been observed in experienced language learners with typologically related languages. From a DST perspective, thus, it can be pointed out that multilingual systems are inherently different from monolingual systems. Additionally, even when the two systems share certain features, they have a different significance in the multilingual system.

1.12 No Boundaries Approach

Herdina and Jessner's (2002) DMM begins to weaken the boundaries among languages by describing them as subsystems included in a multilingual dynamic system. As will be discussed in more detail in the following chapters, a further approach drawing on some concepts of the DST more explicitly questions the possibility of distinguishing and counting languages that compose the multilingual repertoire. Despite sharing several features with the DST, such as the non-linearity and catalytic effect, De Bot's approach departs from it on a crucial aspect (De Bot & Jaensch, 2015). In De Bot and Jaensch's (2015: 141) view, multilingualism should be studied 'as a process', meaning that the different languages should not be studied separately in the repertoire but 'in their interaction over time'. Thus, following the shift of perspective from countable and bounded systems represented in the repertoire to the processual nature of multilingualism, the authors do not highlight any specific features of multilingualism or L3 processing (as opposed to bilingualism or monolingualism).

1.13 Interface Hypothesis

An influential theory which relies on processing factors to explain different outcomes in L2 learners is the Interface Hypothesis (IH), propounded by Sorace (2006, 2011) and colleagues. The theory provides additional evidence of the linguistic and cognitive differences between SLA and TLA, since it has also been extended to L3 learners. Indeed, recent acquisition studies have maintained that interfaces are particularly vulnerable in language acquisition. The IH (Sorace, 2006, 2011; Sorace & Serratrice, 2009) was specifically proposed to account for some of the persistent non-target-like patterns found in adult L2 end-state grammar. The underlying assumption is that different interfaces pose different levels of difficulty in learning L2 properties. In particular, features which involve sub-modules of language (internal interface) are expected to be acquired relatively easier than those relating to cognitive domains (external interface), external to a core computational system.

Since integrating context and grammar requires additional effort by the processor, internal interfaces (such as those between syntax and other linguistic modules) are less problematic than external interfaces for L2 learners. Thus, it was argued that processing difficulties in external interface domains may trigger residual optionality at the end-state grammar of L2 learners. Sorace points out that, in order to better identify and understand the aforementioned optionality as well as the instability found in bilingual speakers at interface conditions, two main factors need to be considered. On the one hand, speakers need to acquire the knowledge of structure and of the mapping conditions that operate within interface components. On the other hand, they also need to acquire the processing principles that apply in the real-time integration of information from different domains.

It has been argued that early research on the IH had taken a restricted perspective on the nature of the interface. Indeed, research mainly focused on the target knowledge representation of structures, rather than on the online processing operations involved in production and comprehension. Instead, the aforementioned two factors discussed by Sorace represent two main accounts: representational and processing resources accounts. They are both particularly relevant for the purpose of the current discussion since they further highlight what differs between monolingual and bilingual speech processing. The first account is based on the assumption that bilinguals and monolinguals are different in how they represent knowledge, in that one of the grammatical systems may affect the other. The second account considers the difference between monolinguals and bilinguals at the level of processing strategies required in the use of interface structures in real time.

Overall, the main reason why bilingual speakers have been reported to perform poorly compared to monolinguals at processing structures, at the syntax–pragmatics interface, is that syntactic processing may be less automatic for them. This can be due to linguistic and/or cognitive factors, i.e. to a less developed knowledge of representation or to less efficient access to these representations. Thus, the IH encouraged an interdisciplinary approach to studies on bilingualism since, as argued, there is no reason to consider linguistic, psychological and neurocognitive research on bilingualism as separate areas that work independently from each other. Instead, the final aim for linguistic theory is 'a full integration of the different levels postulated in the study of the brain/mind' (Rizzi, 2004: 325). Additionally, the IH theory has highlighted the need for a comparison across subfields of bilingual L1, L2 and L3 acquisition as well as attrition. Therefore, it assumes the performance, speech processing mechanisms, learning styles, etc., of bilinguals as a term of comparison in empirical research rather than monolinguals. This leads to a higher degree of empirical reliability in the field, from a methodological point of view, for all the reasons discussed in the course of this chapter, i.e. the overall higher complexity characterising TLA research, the high variability and the number of quantitative and qualitative factors to take into account. For example, the age of acquisition of each language mastered, the number of languages that compose the multilingual repertoire, the amount and type of input received in each language, the status of each language and the motivation.

1.14 Conclusion

This chapter provides an analysis of the most influential theories and models advanced in TLA from a linguistic, psycholinguistic and cognitive perspective, for two main purposes. First, to highlight the complex cognitive nature of multilingual minds which supports the claim that TLA is, inherently, a different process from SLA that needs to be investigated separately in empirical research. Second, to account for the phenomena of transfer, crosslinguistic influence, attrition and other potential factors that can influence the outcome of TLA.

In particular, to demonstrate that TLA is a different area of research from SLA involving specific processes, the most influential speech production and crosslinguistic influence models currently employed in TLA research are compared and contrasted. Regarding speech production models, the issue of how speakers of multiple languages process and understand linguistic inputs is developed starting with the features characterising monolingual and bilingual models. They all contribute to a better understanding of how previous linguistic knowledge affects (by facilitating or complicating) additional language acquisition. Moreover, as already argued, the currently available multilingual speech production models are adaptations of previously developed bilingual models. Hence, further research is needed to explain the inherent mechanism of multilingual minds that takes into account the interaction of different factors following a holistic approach and the higher degree of complexity characterising multilingual speakers.

Concerning the crosslinguistic influence models discussed, it can be noticed that a particular issue taken into account is the economy of linguistic representation. Indeed, the CEM and TPM maintain that L3 learners make use of any previous linguistic knowledge at their disposal to facilitate the task. On the other hand, the L2SF Model assumes that the L2 is more accessible as it is the last language acquired and thus would be more available to building the L3 system. To conclude, TLA needs to be addressed and considered as a separate area of study due to the unique characteristics of additional language learners. The higher number of cognitive and linguistic factors affecting the process and outcome of TLA and the different ways they may combine among each other need to be taken into account with a specific methodological approach and research instruments to obtain a reliable portrait of how multilinguals process and learn additional languages. Hence, in Cenoz's (2004: 8) words, the study of all the factors involved in the process of TLA is potentially more complex than the study of SLA 'because it implicates all the processes associated with SLA as well as unique and potentially more complex relationship that can take place among the languages known or being acquired by the learner'.

2 The Role of Prior Formal Language Learning and Mediating Factors in Third or Additional Language Acquisition

2.1 Introduction

The popular belief among lay speakers that bilinguals are also better additional language learners is also supported by several influential studies in the field of third or additional language acquisition (e.g. Cenoz & Genesee, 1998; Jessner, 1999; Thomas, 1988). However, until a few decades ago, this thesis was not widely accepted in the field of applied linguistics because of several prejudices such as disadvantages, cognitive delay and confusion towards bilingualism on the one hand, and the lack of coherent experimental evidence supporting the controversial issue named 'bilingual advantage' on the other hand.

Nowadays, despite the increasing amount of research on the cognitive and linguistic effects of bilingualism, the literature still shows no consensus on the main factors responsible for bilinguals' better performance when learning additional foreign languages. This chapter initially aims at comparing and contrasting previous and current research on third language acquisition (TLA) in order to determine the extent to which a number of cognitive and affective attributes have a significant impact on the performance of bilinguals when learning any additional language in a formal context. Secondly, among the individual difference factors linked to previous second language (L2) learning, the potential effect of different types of learning, amount of exposure to any previous language, context and age of acquisition, level of bilingualism, literacy and attitude towards the languages will be discussed.

2.2 Attitudes towards Bilingualism: A Historical Perspective

Before a discussion of how each internal and external factor may impact bilinguals' acquisition of additional languages, it is worth recalling that the scientific approach to bilingualism has gone through different historical phases. As already mentioned, previous language knowledge and previous learning experience have not always been regarded as an advantage by all academics. It is commonly agreed that the turning point establishing the beginning of a positive attitude towards bilingualism is 1962, the publication year of Peal and Lambert's (1962) most influential contribution: *The Relation of Bilingualism to Intelligence*.

Before this date, the shared view was that bilingualism even had detrimental effects on cognitive development and, consequently, on the process of learning subsequent languages. Based on this negative perception of the phenomenon, there was the idea that bilingualism was associated with a number of problems in individuals such as speech disorders, cognitive deficits, confusion and intellectual disability (De Angelis, 2007). In his work, Hakuta (1986) argues that during that time, researchers simply assumed, without any doubts, that bilinguals were disadvantaged compared to monolinguals in different cognitive tasks. What differentiated bilinguals was the extent to which being experienced in more than one language could modify their cognitive functions. On the one hand, hereditarians put forward the view that, since intelligence is innate, it could not be modified by experience in other languages. Therefore, individuals who were observed to perform poorly were just considered to have lower IQ scores. On the other hand, environmentalists argued that dealing with more than one language was an obstacle to cognitive development, leading to a number of mental problems and impairments.

Interestingly, Edwards (2004) provides a sociolinguistic explanation in an attempt to find the origins of this prevailing belief among scientists and lay speakers. He noticed that the majority of studies at the time were conducted in the United States, during an era of great social tensions between local populations and immigrants from all over Europe. Specifically, he maintains that research might simply have been misinterpreted to support racial discrimination and restrict the inflow of immigrants into the United States. Indeed, bilingual immigrants were asked to perform tests of intelligence in English, likewise English monolinguals. Therefore, it was not surprising that they recorded lower scores, which placed them in a disadvantaged position. Inevitably, since these studies were also published in the most influential scientific journals of the time, they gained the support of the majority of academics and educators with drastic consequences in terms of educational methodologies. Monolingualism became the norm and any kind of practice of home language by pupils was highly discouraged at school so that it could be totally repressed.

Peal and Lambert's (1962) work started to highlight the weakness of all previous research. It advanced strong and clear methodological arguments to question it, developing the claim that types of bilingualism and the socioeconomic status of the participants had not been properly controlled. Indeed, in their pioneering study on bilingualism and intelligence, the authors compared the performance of monolingual and bilingual children attending school in Canada, examining their cognitive abilities using a number of verbal and non-verbal tasks. What is particularly relevant about the research is that, for the first time, variables such as socioeconomic status and level of proficiency in each language were controlled.

2.3 Bilingual Effects on Cognition and Language Learning: From Representation Analysis to Attentional Control

Starting from the advent of the aforementioned pioneering study by Peal and Lambert in 1962, the approach and methodology of research into bilingualism started to change and improve, taking into account the individual factors characterising bilinguals from different perspectives. Nowadays, there is overwhelming evidence for the notion that bilingualism fosters cognitive development and also facilitates the acquisition of additional languages. However, some negative associations with the bilingual experience can still be found in some specific domains, such as lexical access (Bialystok & Feng, 2009; Gollan et al., 2008; Ivanova & Costa, 2008; Oller & Eilers, 2002).

During the past 20 years, the study of bilingualism from a cognitive point of view has attracted the attention of a large number of researchers focused on the linguistic aspects of a bilingual brain, such as the modality of access to the lexicon and how two or more languages are mastered together. Recently, an increasing number of studies have shifted to the bilingual effect in executive function tasks aimed at assessing whether mastering more than one language has a general effect on basic cognitive, non-verbal skills. Bialystok's (2009) work, for instance, takes into account a number of prominent experiments which demonstrate how bilingualism affects cognitive and linguistic performance across the lifespan in order to provide a general understanding of the different areas where the bilingual experience has been reported to show a positive effect, a negative effect or no effect at all compared to monolinguals. The author points out that individuals who speak an L2 have an increased density of grey matter in the left inferior parietal cortex, the region responsive to vocabulary acquisition in monolinguals and bilinguals. Additionally, being bilingual has also been reported to enhance the so-called cognitive reserve, which is the protective effects against cognitive decline with aging. The main explanation for the generalised cognitive effects of bilingualism comes from Green's (1998) well-known Inhibitory Hypothesis, according to which the non-relevant language is suppressed by the same executive functions involved in the control of attention and inhibition. In other words, it is the constant need to select the target language (TL) meeting both formal and semantic criteria that is responsible for the positive and negative consequences of bilingualism under linguistic and cognitive points of view.

Among the studies where a negative effect of bilingualism has been observed, language proficiency and verbal fluency are the most affected domains due to the bilingual experience, as Bialystok (2009) reports. Indeed, using a variety of tasks such as picture naming, lexical decisions and verbal fluency, bilinguals have shown lower scores compared to monolinguals and have experienced more tips of tongue as well as interferences. One of the possible explanations for bilinguals' deficits in vocabulary access deals with the conflict created by competition from the corresponding item in the non-TL, related to Green's (1998) aforementioned Inhibitory Hypothesis. Another prominent view in the literature argues that bilinguals use each of their languages less often than monolinguals, resulting in weaker connections among the different parts involved in speech production (Michael & Gollan, 2005). Other interpretations consider the age of acquisition of the vocabulary in each language as the most responsible factor, with different outcomes depending on the age of second language acquisition (SLA) (Hernandez & Li, 2007). Finally, Bates and MacWhinney's (1982) Competition Model (CM) can be considered a mechanistic explanation of language acquisition used to account for not only language acquisition but also language comprehension, language production and impaired language processes.

Bialystok's (2009) research on the distinction between control and representational processes sheds light on the differences observed between monolinguals' and bilinguals' performance. Indeed, according to the author, the functions contributing to control processes include selective attention, inhibition and switching between competing alternatives, whereas representational processes concern encoding problems in sufficient detail, accessing relevant information and making logical inferences about relational information. Bialystok's distinction allows associating bilinguals with more effective and faster control processes explained by their constant management of two or more languages. On the contrary, her study does not confirm any relevant difference between bilinguals and monolinguals in representational tasks.

Specifically, she analyses the reason why bilingualism leads to different effects in different types of tasks, i.e. costs in lexical retrieval and benefits in non-verbal tasks. She argues that linguistic and non-linguistic tasks produce different results, despite the involvement of both representation (analysis) and attention (control), because of the different emphasis put on them in each case. Indeed, the fundamental component involved in verbal retrieval is representation, whereas the primary component required in non-verbal tasks is control. According to Bialystok, this explains the general disadvantage for bilinguals in representation and the general advantage in control even though both components are involved. In addition, it is worth noting that there is interaction between these two elements, in that actual cognitive performance cannot be described in terms of relying either on one or the other. This interaction is particularly evident in linguistic tasks where there is a significant demand for executive control, such as verbal fluency tasks.

As already argued, one of the control processes improved by the bilingual experience, particularly relevant in the process of language learning, is the ability to focus and maintain attention more efficiently and for longer periods of time. What is more, this advantage has been confirmed in both early and late bilinguals. Among the factors responsible for the enhanced performance, again, there is the need to control two or more linguistic systems in the brain according to the given linguistic circumstances (i.e. communicative situation, interlocutor's language). On the other hand, from a referential point of view, this ability has been explained by the fact that bilinguals associate at least two different signifiers to concepts resulting in the development of better linguistic awareness.

2.4 Individual Learner Differences Affecting TLA

In regard to individual learner differences (ILD), psychologists have traditionally made a distinction among three concepts. First, cognition refers to how information is processed and learned by humans. Second, conation deals with the way humans use will and freedom to make choices resulting in new behaviours. Third, affect encompasses issues of temperament, emotions and how humans feel towards information, people, objects, actions and thoughts. Nonetheless, contemporary psychologists endorse the need to consider cognitive, conative and affective explanations holistically to fully understand individual differences. Likewise, SLA researchers are increasingly more willing to examine aptitude, motivation and other sources of individual differences in L2 learning in the context of complex interrelationships among cognition, conation and affect (Ortega, 2009: 146). The following sections address the role of three crucial ILD that have been reported to have an impact on TLA: working memory (WM), language aptitude (LA) and motivation.

2.4.1 Working memory

An important cognitive ability improved by the bilingual experience, which plays a fundamental role in the language learning process, is WM. It is considered part of the executive functions skills by some scientists and as an independent skill by others. Baddeley (1992) defines it as a specialised memory system, where small amounts of information can be simultaneously stored and processed for a brief period of time during the performance of a task. The reason why it plays a crucial role in language processing and learning is that it is fundamental in a number of different cognitive tasks where it is necessary to focus the attention, avoid any kind of distraction or interference and overcome any conflicts involved in the information processing. Recent studies have reported superior performance on WM tasks for bilinguals compared to monolinguals, especially in Simon-type tasks focusing on inhibition abilities.

In particular, Linck and Weiss (2011) argue that WM is able to predict the acquisition of explicit knowledge in an L2. Indeed, in their study, they examined whether executive functioning predicts acquisition of explicit L2 knowledge in a classroom context. The data yielded provide convincing evidence that the executive functioning of WM is an important component of L2 aptitude, especially for predicting explicit SLA during the early stages of learning. What makes this longitudinal study particularly significant is that it was the first to demonstrate that a learner's WM can predict L2 learning over time in a classroom context. Moreover, it also suggests that individual differences in WM may have a larger impact on learning than other cognitive processes associated with L2 processing differences such as inhibitory control.

A recent work (Huang et al., 2022) looked at the effects of WM and LA on L2 and third language (L3) learning. Interestingly, it found that the number of languages involved, i.e. two or more, also modulates this effect. More specifically, the research investigated whether LA and WM are changeable under the circumstance of foreign language learning and whether there is an effect of learning two foreign languages simultaneously on these two cognitive abilities. The findings indicated a high degree of changeability of WM and LA. Moreover, a positive effect of learning two foreign languages as opposed to learning just one language on WM development emerged at the early stages of learning a new language. This has been interpreted in terms of constant and intensive learning of two foreign languages simultaneously. Indeed, it involves not only taking in and maintaining new information, but also manipulating and selecting between old and new information.

2.4.2 Language aptitude

The importance of WM started to be highlighted by research into another fundamental factor of foreign language learning, that is LA (Linck et al., 2014; Martin & Ellis, 2012). This complex individual variable, closely related to WM, is not easy to define and measure. The concept was first introduced in the 1960s as an innate, relatively fixed predisposition for language learning, distinct from other traits such as intelligence or motivation. LA used to be considered a componential feature, not modified by training or affected by previous language experience. It is a multifaceted factor that several researchers have attempted to measure through different instruments, with different outcomes and focus on different aspects. Carroll (1981: 86) defined foreign LA as an 'individual's initial state of readiness and capacity for learning a foreign language, and probable degree of facility in doing so'.

Carroll and Sapon (1959) developed the Modern Language Aptitude Test (MLAT) to predict the rate at which an individual would learn a particular language under specific conditions. The four components taken into account are phonetic coding ability, grammatical sensitivity, rate learning ability and inductive learning ability. Another attempt to provide a complete measure of aptitude comes from Pimsleur's (1966) Language Aptitude Battery. The author used the empirically based psychometric approach administering various tests that seemed to predict language learning success and then selected the tasks that best differentiated between successful and unsuccessful learners. However, the most striking flaw of the experiment was the lack of a theoretical foundation because the nature of the phenomenon in question was not clearly defined. One of the most successful attempts to overcome this weakness comes from the Cognitive Ability for Novelty in Acquisition (CANAL-F), a theory-based aptitude test.

Nowadays, researchers take into account cognitive and perceptive factors (e.g. Doughty *et al.*, 2010) and consider LA as a complex cluster of interactive variables. In Robinson's (2002) view, for example, LA is not a fixed characteristic of the learner but rather a complex reflection of the whole learning situation including instructional conditions and type of language exposure. The Aptitude Complex Hypothesis, proposed by Robinson, is based on the seminal work of the late educational psychologist Richard Snow (1987, 1994). It is grounded in the assumption that clusters of traits coming together, due to interactional and mutual support, have better predictive powers than traits considered in isolation. More specifically, in Snow's work, three principles are highlighted: (a) human aptitude is made up of a complex of abilities, interrelated in a hierarchical fashion rather than a simple or direct fashion; (b) differential cognitive processing abilities are intertwined with the contexts and affordances of the environment; and (c) differential aptitude cannot be fully explained unless motivational and affective influences are taken into account as well.

In his theory, Robinson (2002, 2005: 51) emphasises the first two principles, claiming that 'abilities [...] have their effects in combination of "complexes" [...] which jointly facilitate processing and learning in a specific instructional context'. In particular, in his view, the two aptitude complexes explaining why some learners are better than others at benefiting from recasts are 'noticing the gap' and 'memory for contingent speech'. The first occurs when the learner compares their own utterance to the one heard from the interlocutor whereas the second occurs when the learner actually remembers the utterance of the interlocutor to such an extent as to rehearse it in memory or to recognise it in future.

Skehan (2015), on the other hand, added a temporal dimension to the construct of LA suggesting that particular skills and cognitive abilities become essential at various stages of language acquisition. That is to say, aspects of LA change and adapt in response to changing environmental demands and a growing level of L2 proficiency activates different aptitude components. For example, it has been argued that phonetic coding ability is very important at the initial stages of learning, whereas grammatical sensitivity starts to be activated later on. Hence, in Skehan's opinion, aptitude can be described as a fixed identity that changes qualitatively but not quantitatively. To put it another way, it changes according to the different stages of the acquisitional micro processes rather than at the beginning or ending phase of the learning process. Interestingly, Robinson (2005) recognises that motivational and affective forces also influence the way a number of basic cognitive abilities and aptitude complexes work in different conditions. That is, individuals who are highly motivated may learn faster and better because they may take every encounter in the L2 as an opportunity for learning.

2.4.3 Motivation

As discussed, aptitude is a complex construct including many cognitive abilities and helps explain why people differ in terms of speed and achievement levels when learning languages. Nonetheless, cognitive abilities alone cannot fully explain individual differences. According to Ortega (2009):

> since humans are conscious and volitional creatures, in explaining perception, behaviour and learning, we also need to account for human intentions, goals, plans and commitments. These are conative influences that at the broadest level include volition and motivation, and they can make language learners succeed or fail. (Ortega, 2009: 168)

Early motivation research focused on measuring the amount of motivation of individuals during the process of learning a foreign language and on determining whether this measured quantity predicted their achievement level. However, to understand language learning motivation, it is crucial to identify the variables contributing to increasing or decreasing its level. These variables are known as antecedents or 'motivational substrates' that give form to the structure of motivation. Integrativeness has been recognised as the antecedent that plays a central role in foreign language motivation. Gardner (2001: 5) defines it as 'a genuine interest in learning the second language in order to come closer to the other language community'. It involves three dimensions: favourable attitudes towards L2 speakers; general interest in foreign languages and low ethnocentricism; endorsement of reasons for learning the L2 related to interaction with L2 members or, in Gardner's terms, an 'integrative orientation'. Interestingly, Gardner (2001) identifies 'integrative motivation' as the highest and most facilitative form of motivation. Three conditions are required for it to occur: (1) the antecedent of integrativeness itself is high; (2) motivation quantity (i.e. the combined amount of effort, enjoyment and investment) is also high; and (3) attitudes towards the learning situation (i.e. teachers, curriculum) are positive. Indeed, Gardner (2001) asserted that exceptionally successful learners who attain native-like competence are likely to be integratively motivated individuals.

Among the other antecedents of motivation, it is worth considering orientations and attitudes. Orientations refer to the reasons that prompt learners to take up a particular language whereas attitudes refer to the disposition towards the L2 community as well as its speakers. In an instructional setting, it refers to the attitude towards teachers and curriculum. Orientations affect motivation in that they set the goal of learning a particular language. They can be multiple and support motivation at different levels. Individuals may show several orientations at the same time. Ortega (2009) reports the different orientations for learning a language that L2 learners exhibit across different contexts: instrumental (e.g. getting a better job or pursuing a higher level of education in the L2); for knowledge or enlightened understanding of one's own identity, language or culture and to become a more knowledgeable person; to facilitate travel to other countries; for fostering general friendship with members of the TL; for integrative reasons related to identification with the target culture and a genuine desire to become more like members of the L2 group.

Among the reasons leading people to learn additional languages, attitudes towards that particular language and its speakers are likely to affect the levels of motivation. They are the result of collective values, beliefs, attitudes and even behaviours of learners in the communities where they act and participate. The latter may be a classroom, family or the wider social environment and institutions. In other words, they constitute the 'sociocultural milieu'. Considering the crucial role played by affective factors, specifically attitude, in language acquisition, it is worth discussing the implications of this factor from an educational perspective. A study by Portolés (2014) looked at the effects of teachers' attitudes towards three languages. The main aim of the research, conducted in the Valencian community, was to investigate prospective teachers' attitudes towards the majority language Spanish, the minority language Catalan and the foreign language English. Moreover, the effects of the sociolinguistic contexts and the mother tongue were considered. An interesting and unexpected finding is that there were no statistical differences between the sociolinguistic context and language attitudes towards Catalan, the minority language. This seems to suggest that the sociolinguistic context is of paramount importance in determining language attitudes. Indeed, the asymmetric multilingualism that characterises the Valencian community is mirrored in the different linguistic attitudes recorded, based on the region of origin. Students in Castelló, for instance, tended to be more protective towards the minority language whereas students in Valencia were more open to all three languages included in the study.

The mother tongue, on the other hand, was another factor affecting prospective teachers' attitudes towards the languages. They tended to show more favourable attitudes towards certain languages with which they felt more familiar. Nonetheless, no relationship was found between the home language and English, the international foreign language included. Indeed, most participants showed a positive attitude towards English despite having Spanish as their L1. The author suggests that further research is needed to better understand the effect of the mother tongue on language attitude towards English. Hence, the implication of this study is that acknowledging the importance of attitude in language education, starting from the analysis of teachers' positive attitude, may have a strong impact on developing students' attitudes towards languages in the future.

From the point of view of students' motivation affecting TLA, it is worth recalling a study by Khan *et al.* (2020) that explored the learning of Chinese as an L3 in educational contexts, i.e. different foreign language institutes in Delhi, India. The study examined the motivation, purpose, strategy, attitude and problems of Indian students in Chinese language acquisition. Based on primary research data collected through questionnaires, it was found that instrumental motivation is the sole reason behind third foreign language acquisition in India, and it also positively influences the proficiency level in that language.

Motivation, on the other hand, or 'emotional investment' (Kinginger, 2008; Norton, 2001) is an affective factor growing in any direction depending on how individuals with their unique personalities and preferences react to the pedagogical, social, historical, political and cultural environment. Individual contexts are inextricably linked to social contexts, that is, the intergroup climate in which interlocutors evolve and which has a stable, long-term influence on the learner (e.g. intergroup relations, gender, social class) (MacIntyre *et al.*, 1998). Language prestige constitutes one of the reasons influencing why learners may be more or less attracted to particular languages. To better understand this concept, it is worth recalling Fishman's (1966) distinction between folk and elite bilingualism, related to the prestige and social status of the languages involved. The folk are immigrants and linguistic minorities who exist within the milieu of a dominant language that is not their own and whose own language is not held in high esteem within society. The elite are those who speak the dominant language and whose societal status is enhanced through the mastery of additional languages.

Hence, heritage languages (HLs) considered by the community and social environment as less prestigious are less likely to be learned and taught even in multilingual contexts. That is, the sociolinguistic and learning situation where language acquisition takes place seems to be crucial in the analysis of language attitudes and motivation in multilingual communities. According to Baker (2000), the level of support for bilingualism and bilingual education, and the inhabitants' attitudes towards them, are crucial in determining the linguistic situation of a country. This latter, in turn, affects the perceptions, feelings and dispositions of speakers towards the languages. In other words, it can be argued that these factors influence each other and determine the sociolinguistic context of a particular country where different languages may coexist as majority, minority and/or foreign languages.

2.5 The 'Bilingual Advantage' in Third Language Acquisition

From the analysis of the most prominent literature provided so far, there is ample support to claim that being bilingual leads to advantages in a number of different cognitive and linguistic tasks. In particular, the last decade has witnessed a considerable increase in interest in the benefits of bilingualism in the field of third or additional language acquisition. However, if on the one hand it is widely acknowledged that bilingualism fosters cognition and thus the language acquisition process on a general level, on the other, the nature and extent to which each specific variable affects the outcome in TLA remain a matter of debate.

As De Angelis (2007) points out, at least three common hypotheses have been put forward by academics concerning the factors responsible for bilinguals' better performance when learning foreign languages. The first is that an individual's knowledge of more languages facilitates and increases the speed and efficiency of the learning process thanks to the enhancement of cognitive development. An alternative hypothesis found in the literature is that additional language knowledge does not represent a significant difference in the language acquisition process. Indeed, it seems that bilinguals are better and more efficient than monolinguals on a general level but they are essentially similar in the way they acquire languages. Finally, there is a further hypothesis claiming that additional language knowledge may be detrimental to the other languages known by a speaker.

All these views take into account two fundamental elements which need to be distinguished. First, there is the effect that knowledge of previous languages has on cognitive development, including the aforementioned skills such as problem-solving, attention and memory. Second, there is the effect that previous language knowledge and experience has on the acquisition process itself. In other words, the discussion focuses on whether these factors may have a significant impact on the level of proficiency and grammar accuracy in a third or additional language. As far as the effects of prior language knowledge on foreign language achievement are concerned, two main critical questions have been raised by previous literature, known as the 'Threshold Hypothesis' and the 'Developmental

Interdependence Hypothesis', both formulated by Cummins (1976, 1979). The first deals with the level of proficiency that the learner must reach in one language to be able to benefit from the so-called bilingual advantage. In particular, it suggests the existence of two different threshold levels of linguistic competence. If learners reach the first level, they will be able to avoid any cognitive disadvantage associated with bilingualism. The second level is necessary for the positive effects of bilingualism on improved executive functions to occur.

The 'threshold level' of linguistic competence allows learners to avoid cognitive deficits as well as to exploit the potential aspects of becoming bilingual. The Developmental Interdependence Hypothesis, on the other hand, states that the linguistic competencies achieved by the learner in an L2 are partly due to the competencies already developed in the L1, since they can be transferred and used to learn additional languages.

Another relevant observation provided by Cummins is that the experience of becoming bilingual can positively influence aspects of cognitive functioning as a result of either home or school experience. This lends support to two main claims: first, learning languages in a formal educational environment has an impact on cognitive growth; and second, bilingual language experience in a school setting may be more capable of influencing divergent than convergent thinking skills. Cummins' (1976, 1979) theories allow us to investigate in more detail the effect of two crucial variables on TLA: the level of bilingualism, i.e. the level of proficiency reached in each language mastered by the speaker, and the role of the different contexts of acquisition.

2.6 Level of Bilingualism: The Role of Proficiency in L3 Learning Performance

In another influential paper, Roehr (2008) specifically looks at the correlation between proficiency in an L2 and metalinguistic knowledge in L1 English learners of German as an L2. She points out that knowledge of grammar and vocabulary as evident in a proficient L2 performance may not only be built up on the basis of explicitly acquired metalinguistic knowledge but may also help a learner develop their metalinguistic knowledge in the first place. In other words, she argues that knowledge about knowledge may arise from language competence (i.e. proficiency) rather than the other way round. Additionally, the author raises further important questions, such as the extent to which metalinguistic description explanation ability may have different roles to play at different levels of L2 proficiency. She suggests that in order to investigate the cause–effect relationship between explanation and language analytic abilities, it is necessary to compare several proficiency levels through a longitudinal study assessing whether metalinguistic knowledge about specific features is constructed on the basis of L2 knowledge.

One of the most interesting approaches in the field comes from the work by Cenoz and Valencia (1994) that considered the influence of bilingualism on L3 learning, comparing Basque/Spanish bilinguals learning English as an L3. Assuming the Interdependence Hypothesis as a starting point (Cummins, 1981), they report that if instruction in one language is effective in promoting proficiency in that language, the transfer of this proficiency to another language will occur provided there is enough exposure and motivation. What is particularly remarkable about the study is that it also controls for the potential influence of a number of mediating variables, i.e. linguistic, sociolinguistic, psychological and educational. Indeed, this is of crucial importance if one takes into account the complexity of the phenomena of bilingualism and TLA as well as the number of aforementioned factors which affect them.

Participants' performance in the L3 was assessed through five different tests of English to measure different dimensions of proficiency, i.e. four tests of language skills (speaking, listening, reading, writing) and a multiple choice test of vocabulary and grammar. In agreement with previous studies, the findings showed that first, bilingualism has a positive mediating effect on TLA; second, the regression analysis demonstrated that the inclusion of bilingualism significantly improved the effects of other predictors; and third, most importantly, there were no interaction effects between bilingualism and other predictors. This means that the effects of bilingualism were obtained regardless of the effects of cognitive, sociocultural and psychological variables. Accordingly, the experiments confirm the claim proposed by Swain *et al.* (1990) that literacy in a HL is associated with higher levels of achievement in an L3.

Another contribution investigating the impact that the level of proficiency in an L2 has on the acquisition of a third or additional language comes from Jaensch (2009). The three languages involved in the research were Japanese (L1), English (L2) and German (L3). The significance of the study relies on the fact that not only does it demonstrate that L3 learners perform better than monolinguals in terms of the proficiency of both general and specific features, but it also raises the question of whether the proficiency level in an L2 can affect the performance of a specific element in the L3 which is absent in the participants' L1 and L2.

Notably, the results indicate that, despite the fact that grammatical gender is not marked on determiners in English, participants with similar proficiency in German but higher proficiency in English L2 performed better in the gender assignment task. However, it is worth underlining that this beneficial effect is not recorded at all proficiency levels and for all features. To interpret these findings, the authors resort to two different theories: the Additive Effect of Bilingualism Hypothesis and the already mentioned Threshold Hypothesis. The first is fully supported by the results since those L3 learners of German with higher proficiency in English L2 outperformed learners with similar levels of German but lower proficiency in the L2. The second is only partially confirmed by the study as, on the one hand, lower intermediate learners of German (L3) did not show considerable effect of L2 English proficiency on the detection of gender, and in the case of the determiner, on the other hand, the L2 higher proficiency effect was evident on the same features but on the attributive adjective.

However, in order to fully confirm or disconfirm the two hypotheses, larger groups of participants are needed and, in particular, regarding the Threshold Hypothesis, it would be worth observing a more heterogeneous group including lower proficiencies in the L2. On the basis of the evidence provided, the author suggests that learners of an L3 exhibit more refined metalinguistic awareness (MLA), a wider lexical knowledge and more developed cognitive skills, making them more sensitive to new features in the L3. Jaensch has named this skill 'enhanced feature sensitivity', which is responsible for helping L3 learners to trigger the setting of Universal Grammar (UG) parameters.

A similar account is provided by Klein's (1995) study. She compared monolingual and multilingual schoolchildren in the acquisition of specific properties in lexical and syntactic learning. The previous languages of the multilinguals varied but all were very similar to English in the manner in which Wh-questions are formed; specifically, none of them allows preposition stranding. The multilingual group significantly outperformed the monolinguals both in correct sub-categorisation and preposition stranding. The author concluded that the attitude to learning, the heightened metalinguistic skills and the enhanced lexical knowledge and cognitive skills of multilinguals are all advantageous in triggering the setting of UG parameters.

The studies reviewed, taking into account the role of proficiency developed in an L2, provide additional evidence to support the claim that bilingualism fosters additional language learning. However, it is important to maintain that proficiency in any language cannot be considered as a static element since it may change over time and is affected by a number of other factors, as suggested by the models reviewed in Chapter 1. Moreover, when dealing with proficiency, it is crucial to separately assess the effects of knowledge of the language and knowledge about the language, as explained in the following sections.

2.7 Implicit and Explicit Language Learning and Knowledge

Language learning is a complex cognitive phenomenon involving different factors. It is possible to distinguish the factors into two main categories: cognitive and individual. Among the most relevant cognitive variables, together with the level of memory and intelligence, the learning strategies developed through a particular type and amount of exposure to previous languages play a fundamental role. Hence, recent research into the field of language acquisition seems to validate the importance of distinguishing between two different types of learning, i.e. implicit and explicit, since they seem to lead to the development of different types of knowledge.

A number of fundamental skills rely on implicit knowledge such as social interaction, music perception, intuitive decision-making as well as language comprehension and production. In particular, when dealing with TLA research, awareness of these fundamental skills is of crucial importance to understand the way they interact and the extent to which they affect the process of learning additional languages. Arthur Reber (1967: 317–327) was first to employ this terminology, defining implicit learning as 'a process during which subjects derive knowledge from a complex, rule-governed stimulus domain without intending to and without becoming aware of the knowledge they have acquired'. In regard to the term explicit, it is usually employed in learning environments where subjects are instructed to actively look for patterns. In other words, learning is an intentional process resulting from conscious knowledge. Reber's (1993) theory of the primacy of implicit processes has been extended to the development of MLA. He maintains that implicit processes developed earlier in the human evolution and are less subject to variation. On the other hand, explicit processes show much greater flexibility, are more trainable, faster and develop to a greater extent. That is why, when focusing on form, the patterns of grammar are more likely to be internalised.

The most prominent contribution to the characterisation of implicit and explicit knowledge comes from Krashen's (1982) work, where he refers to this fundamental distinction employing different terms, i.e. 'acquisition' and 'learning'. The first is described as an incidental process resulting in tacit linguistic knowledge, whereas the second is an intentional process that results in conscious, metalinguistic knowledge. He points out that conscious learning of language and subconscious acquisition of it are completely different. This provides evidence that L2 students of grammar-translation methods with a technical knowledge of the grammar, which is even superior to native speakers of that language, are not necessarily fluent in conversational skills.

On the role of noticing, Truscott and Sharwood Smith (2011) argue that it should be important for the acquisition of metalinguistic knowledge but it should not play a direct role in the development of the language module. More specifically, regarding the role of consciousness in the input–intake relationship, they put forward an interpretation in terms of the interdisciplinary framework called Modular Online Growth and Use of Language (MOGUL): 'a representation becomes conscious if and only if its activation level crosses a threshold (the activation hypothesis). The representations that can attain such levels are those in perceptual output structures and those in affective structures' (Truscott & Sharwood Smith, 2011: 524).

The implicit–explicit relationship has also been defined as the 'Interface Question in SLA' (Ellis, 2011). It is crucial to understanding the origins of the different theses put forward by academics on the role played by instruction in language learning. To portray the issue in Ellis' (2011) terms, the most evident difference between explicit and implicit knowledge is that children are able to acquire their L1 from their caretakers in a naturalistic setting without any particular effort. On the one hand, they are able to acquire complex knowledge of the structure of that language, and on the other, they are not able to describe the different patterns of the linguistic structure and the mechanism on the basis of its working. Thus, it can be argued that, first, the acquisition of L1 grammar is implicit and derives from experience rather than from explicit rules, and second, no explicit instruction is needed. Adult acquisition of foreign languages is a completely different matter since what can be acquired in a spontaneous environment is quite limited in comparison to native speakers' norms. Additionally, to reach a certain accuracy level usually requires the support of additional conscious explicit knowledge.

These different conceptions of the nature of language representation and acquisition have led to different teaching methods. The supporters of a rule-governed way of teaching languages developed teaching programmes based on grammar and form, motivated by the idea that before using a language it is necessary to be aware of its rules. 'Focus-on-form' (FonF), for example, is a central construct in task-based language teaching. The expression, introduced by Long (1991), refers to an approach where learners' attention is attracted to linguistic forms as they engage in the performance of tasks. It differs from a structure-based approach – 'Focus-on-forms' (FonFs) – where specific linguistic forms are taught directly and explicitly. On the other hand, the so-called 'communicative' or natural approach is grounded in the assumption that adult language learning is implicit, like L1 acquisition. Since this approach maintains that language skills and having knowledge about language are different matters, it denies the value of any explicit grammar-based instruction.

From the aforementioned premises on acquisition and learning advanced by Krashen (1982), three important considerations can be made. First, there is no strong interface between explicit and implicit knowledge; second, they are not connected in any way in the process of learning/acquisition; and third, 'acquisition' (i.e. implicit learning) is, in fact, the only one leading to development in any foreign language since the role of 'learning' (i.e. explicit learning) only works as a monitor to avoid mistakes during the production of utterances. Accordingly, he argues that it is necessary to create the conditions for language acquisition to take place since L2 development is mainly the result of unconscious acquisition facilitated by meaning alone. On the other hand, explicit learning, that is the conscious attempt to look for grammatical rules, only leads to the development of a peripheral system which is independent of the acquired system.

Despite being criticised for not giving enough importance to the role of grammatical skills and MLA, Krashen's model paved the way for an intense debate on the controversial issue of the role and nature of explicit and implicit learning. Indeed, on the basis of empirical analysis of learners attending communicative (grammar-free) programmes, researchers started to highlight the limits of the accuracy of their language performance. Consequently, this empirical evidence together with the critical theoretical disagreement with Krashen's hypothesis, prompted Schmidt (1990) to propound a further theory. That is, conscious cognitive effort, where noticing is involved, constitutes the necessary condition for the conversion of input into foreign language acquisition to occur. In other words, learners in all learning conditions who claim to notice the rules should outperform those who do not, in that conscious noticing is necessary for subsequent learning. But does the level of awareness developed during training affect the extent of learning equally in all conditions? According to Robinson (1997), the answer to this question is yes, depending on the level of participants' awareness.

Krashen's (1982) claim has also been questioned by a number of studies (i.e. De Graaf, 1997; De Keyser, 1995; Robinson, 1997) which probed that L2 learning in explicit conditions, involving some degree of MLA and instruction, was at least as effective as learning in implicit conditions even where the stimulus domain was complex. Therefore, the demonstrable role of noticing in second (or additional) language acquisition gradually led to a rejection of the extreme non-interface position. Within the field of applied linguistics, there were supporters of some form of weak interface position (e.g. Ellis, 1994; Long, 1991). According to this sort of middle-ground position, explicit instruction plays different roles, especially in the perception of the L2 form by facilitating the process of noticing the input, i.e. paying attention to specific linguistic features. The supporters of the weak interface brought the attention back to the role of explicit instruction. However, this did not translate into decontextualised and meaningless exercises, which come under the definition of 'focus-on-form' (Long, 1991). Instead, instruction started to be integrated into meaningful communicative contexts where learners' errors were corrected in the course of naturalistic conversation rather than through negative evidence only relying upon explicit FonF.

Observing participants' behaviour in artificial learning (ALL) tasks, Dienes (2004, 2008) tried to dissociate conscious and unconscious knowledge and she concluded that two kinds of knowledge characterise ALL: structural and judgment knowledge. In the test phase, people use their structural knowledge to form a new piece of knowledge whereas the understanding of whether a particular test item has the same structure as the training items is part of judgment knowledge. The author argues that both can be conscious or unconscious and that conscious structural knowledge leads to conscious judgment knowledge; however, if structural knowledge is unconscious, judgment knowledge can be either conscious or unconscious. Going back to natural languages, these interesting observations shed light on the difference between structural linguistic knowledge, which is unconscious, and metalinguistic judgment knowledge, which is conscious. This explains why even people who feel confident in making grammatical decisions are not necessarily able to explain the reasons for their choices.

It has been argued that there are a number of psychological processes by which explicit knowledge of form-meaning associations has an impact on implicit language learning. The role of consciousness supports the weak interface position with the focus on explicit instruction. Indeed, it has been considered of crucial importance in L2 learning by means of 'noticing the gap' and guided output practice. According to Ellis (2005), the interface, like consciousness, is dynamic, situated and decontextualised: it happens transiently during conscious processing, but the influence upon implicit cognition endures.

Schmidt (2001) maintains that since many features of L2 input are likely to be infrequent, non-salient and communicatively redundant, intentionally focused attention may be a practical necessity for successful language learning. Terrell (1991) points out that explicit instruction is targeted at increasing the salience of commonly ignored features by providing meaningful input that contains the same grammatical meaning–form relationship. Moreover, as regards the 'noticing the gap' process, it has been argued that a learner's output can prompt negative feedback in the form of a corrective recast (Long, 2006), i.e. the reformulation of a spontaneous utterance replacing non-target items with corresponding TL forms. The importance of a recast is to present the learner with psycholinguistic data optimised for acquisition since it makes the gap evident. As far as the role of output practice is concerned, experimental findings support the effectiveness of encouraging learners to produce output in SLA (e.g. De Keyser *et al.*, 2002; Norris & Ortega, 2000). Explicit memories guide the conscious building of novel linguistic utterances through the process of an analogy of formulas as well as of pedagogical grammar rules, which bring a conscious creation of utterances. Afterwards, through use, the move from declarative to procedural knowledge occurs.

Although much of L1 acquisition involves implicit learning, the same mechanisms do not suffice for second (or additional) language learning because of learned attention and transfer from the L1. That is why SLA must overcome the processes of the L1 employing additional resources of explicit learning. Thus, to sum up, the interface between explicit and implicit knowledge is dynamic; consciousness plays a number of different roles in SLA, including learners' noticing negative evidence (i.e. 'noticing the gap'), their attending to language form, their perception, focused by explicit instruction and their voluntary use of grammatical descriptive and analogical reasoning. In other words, consciousness represents the interface by creating access to the vast amount of unconscious resources of knowledge broadcast through the brain.

2.8 The Role of Literacy in Prior Languages

Many definitions of literacy focus on the ability to read and write at an appropriate level. For example, Blake and Hanley (1995: 89) claim: 'The attribute of literacy is generally recognised as one of the key educational objectives of compulsory schooling. It refers to the ability to read and write to an appropriate level of fluency'. However, since it is not possible to provide an objective definition of what 'an appropriate level', 'effectively' or 'well' mean, it follows that there is no commonly accepted definition of literacy. Hence, '[t]here is no universal standard of literacy' (Lawton & Gordon, 1996: 138).

As already mentioned, a particular question of interest discussed by Swain *et al.* (1990) was the impact on L3 learning of HL use which includes literacy compared to HL use which does not include literacy. Results showed that literacy in the HL has a strong positive impact on learning French as an L3 in the bilingual programme, whereas HL use without literacy has little effect. The learning of L2 literacy skills is enhanced through having developed such skills in the L1.

However, only a few studies examine the impact of L1 literacy knowledge and use on L3 learning. The effect of L1 literacy has been reported *per se*, independently of L1 oral language skills, the general level of proficiency and the typological proximity between the two languages. The main limitation of the study is that it is not known when the HL students learned to undertake literacy activities in their HL. For some participants, it is highly probable that they learned these skills in HL programmes at school. This means that, for them, HL might not be their language of initial literacy. However, what is remarkable is that HL literacy provides them with a broader understanding of 'what reading and writing are for, using the medium of a language that [they] speak fluently' (Hudelson, 1987: 830). Additionally, it may help to enhance their pride and self-confidence, which, as the authors suggest, may breed further success and linguistic interdependence.

Another contribution looking at the specific role of literacy comes from Cristina Sanz (2000), who investigated the relationship between biliteracy in a minority and majority language, i.e. Catalan and Spanish, and the acquisition of English as a foreign language (EFL). In this research, apart from separating the effects of biliteracy and bilingualism, a number of predicting factors in the acquisition of additional languages were also controlled, such as intelligence, motivation and sociolinguistic status. Additionally, despite not having operationalised the effect of cognitive variables including WM and MLA, the study suggests interesting hypotheses on the basis of previous studies' results, which explain the advantages of bilinguals over monolinguals in TLA.

Referring to the weak interface position in SLA theory (Ellis, 1994), Sanz (2000) propounds the view that if it is not possible for explicit knowledge to be transformed into implicit knowledge of the L2, it can still help in the acquisition process by acting as an advanced organiser, focusing learners' attention on the relevant features of the language. Indeed, she states that bilingualism may naturally show the behaviour that different researchers working within the FonF tradition (i.e. Doughty & Williams, 1998) are trying to induce in classroom language learners. Thus, it can be argued that literacy encourages MLA on account of language being turned into a visual medium. That is, readers focus on form and improve their memory skills, their aesthetic function as well as their reifying function, i.e. the meaning no longer resides in the speaker but in the text (Kemp, 2001). Writing, in particular, provides the means for analysing language because it turns the language into a visual object. Therefore, literacy is fundamental in the development of MLA in that it allows people to make language visible.

An interesting study by Haim (2014) looked at a number of important factors predicting academic proficiency (AP) among Russian-speaking (L1) immigrants currently studying Hebrew as an L2 and English as an L3 in Israeli schools. Indeed, the work analysed the contribution of demographic, linguistic and social-psychological variables, as well as the AP level in the L1, L2 and L3 to the prediction of AP in the L2 and L3. The results indicated that gender, arrival age, current language use, perceived parental aspirations, L3 writing ability and studying the L1 at school significantly predicted AP in the L2. On the other hand, in regard to the AP in the L3, only age at onset, current language use and L2 writing ability played a significant role. Writing ability in the L1 was a significant predictor of reading and writing abilities in both the L2 and L3, even after controlling for all background variables.

Once acknowledged that biliteracy enhances MLA and, consequently, the process of language learning itself, it is worth pointing out that even a limited amount of formal L2 learning helps to develop the aforementioned metalinguistic skills. Indeed, an interesting study by Yelland *et al.* (1993) appears to validate such a view since it proved that advanced bilingualism is not necessary for a learner's metalinguistic skill to develop. In other words, even limited contact with an L2 can have beneficial effects, which have been observed to carry on into the acquisition of literacy. In particular, the work examined the effects of marginal bilingualism on MLA on the basis of reading acquisition skills. Two sets of English native speakers were tested, one of which studied Italian for one hour per week. The results showed a causal relationship between six months of language learning and increased rates of reading acquisition, measured according to word awareness skills.

2.9 Early and Late Bilingualism: The Role of Age of Acquisition of Previous Languages

A number of controversial issues, largely debated among scholars, on the benefits of bilingualism in the acquisition of any additional language, concern the age of acquisition and the type and amount of instruction that bilinguals must have in the L2 in order to show an advantage in the process and outcome of learning an additional language. After comparing previous research in the field, Rothman (2015) argues in an influential paper that early bilinguals outperform late bilinguals in TLA thanks to the fact that they have two activated grammatical systems developed from an early age. On the other hand, Jaensch's (2012) view rests on the assumption that there are more advantages for learners of an L3 if their L2 experience begins at an older age since they have access to a more enhanced MLA in contrast to the more implicit learning environment of younger learners.

A longitudinal study by Pfenninger and Singleton (2016) looked at the interaction of age with the role of knowledge of other languages in oral and written tasks completed by the same student cohort of 200 Swiss learners of EFL over a period of five years. The following aspects were considered: the short- and long-term effects of an early start on crosslinguistic influence; the roles of the L1 and the L2 in L3 acquisition; and the role of TL proficiency in the acquisition of lexico-semantic and morphosyntactic features. An interesting aspect to highlight about the research is that it included other potential predictors beyond biological age, age of onset (AO) and TL proficiency. Specifically, the study also addressed the perceived and assumed language proximity between the source and the TL, MLA and the influence of the learning environment. From the analyses obtained, a significant effect of TL proficiency, MLA and contextual factors such as class effects, teaching practices and class size were observed.

Cenoz (2001) presents similar findings in her study on crosslinguistic influence in TLA. The results concerning the relationship between crosslinguistic influence and age indicate that older learners show more crosslinguistic influence than younger learners. According to the author, this is due to the higher MLA developed by older students which allows them to perceive the typological distance of the languages involved and to choose which one is the most suitable to use as a source of transfer when acquiring a foreign language. Specifically, the older participants involved in the study were reported to transfer more words from Spanish than Basque when learning English as an L3 since they were aware of the linguistic distance. On the other hand, younger participants with a lower degree of MLA used both Spanish and Basque terms as a source of transfer since they were not able to perceive the objective linguistic distance.

In another work, it has been claimed that both early and late bilinguals have benefits in TLA following different routes and learning strategies (Park & Starr, 2016). Indeed, if on the one hand early bilingualism is achieved in a more implicit language learning environment, it is also true that learners can access two more developed grammatical systems. On the other hand, late bilingualism is more explicit in that it facilitates the acquisition of formal rules in a subsequent language. In other words, both explanations account for enhanced levels of MLA with the difference concerning the routes of acquisition and the particular kind of fundamental cognitive skill.

On the mediating role of MLA, it is worth reporting the results of a study by Huang (2016) that looked at the effects of language characteristics on the development of MLA and, in turn, at the effects observed in third or additional language performance.

2.10 Conclusion

To conclude, the examination of the different research contributions highlights that TLA is characterised by a high number of both internal and external factors that need to be considered holistically to thoroughly understand the peculiar nature of the learning process itself as well as the unique profile of third or additional language learners. Both cognitive and affective attributes have a significant impact on the performance of bilinguals when learning any additional language in a formal context. Accordingly, it would be reductive to provide a unique answer to explain the extent to which individual, external, cognitive and affective variables affect the process and outcomes of TLA. That is, the relationship between different types of learning, amount of exposure to any previous language, context and age of acquisition, level of bilingualism, literacy and attitude towards the languages need to be considered following an interdisciplinary approach.

Moreover, the chapter shows how the methodological approach and the research aptitude towards bilingualism have changed considerably through history. The prejudices concerning the linguistic and cognitive disadvantage of bilingualism were overcome in favour of a more positive and inclusive approach to additional language learning from an educational perspective too. From a cognitive point of view, there are still ongoing debates in the literature discussing the so-called 'bilingual advantage'. Nonetheless, as discussed, the apparent contradictions of research findings can be resolved looking at the specific factors observed, i.e. analysis of representation and control of attention, what is meant by 'bilingual' when recruiting participants and a broader interpretation of the findings which goes beyond the categorical dichotomies between bilinguals and monolinguals. Hence, to sum up, all these considerations taken together suggest that what supports bilinguals in additional language learning is the knowledge of previous languages both in terms of the learning process, strategies and the transfer of lexical and morphosyntactic patterns between L1/L2 and L3/Ln. This is particularly evident when the languages included in the linguistic repertoire of bilingual learners belong to the same typological category. However, it should be borne in mind that the qualitative and quantitative differences characterising the cognitive and linguistic profile of third or additional language learners need to be considered from a holistic perspective to obtain a reliable portrait of how different languages interact among each other and may enhance the process and outcomes of TLA.

3 Metalinguistic Awareness and Third or Additional Language Acquisition

3.1 Introduction

Multilingual acquisition is a non-linear and complex dynamic process affected by a number of factors, selectively discussed in Chapter 2, that interact and influence the variability of the process. Among these factors, it is crucial to consider the particular profile of the third language (L3) learner, learner proficiency, linguistic domain, grammatical features and the relation between previous and additional languages and language (psycho)typology (e.g. Cabrelli Amaro & Rothman, 2010; Cenoz & Valencia, 1994; Gallardo del Puerto, 2007; Gibson *et al.*, 2001; Llama *et al.*, 2010; Pittman, 2008; Ringbom, 2001). Yet, as already mentioned, another factor playing a fundamental role in third language acquisition (TLA), especially from the recent perspective of the Dynamic Model of Multilingualism (DMM) (Herdina & Jessner, 2002), is the linguistic background of the learner in relation to their literacy in the second language (L2), and more specifically, their metalinguistic knowledge (MLK) and awareness (De Bot & Jaensch, 2015). This chapter focuses on the relationship between metalinguistic awareness (MLA) and previous language learning experience in order to investigate how they can be conceptualised, their development and the way they relate and affect each other. In particular, the development of MLA will be described taking into account the different aspects characterising this complex and dynamic phenomenon on the one hand and its influence on the acquisition of additional languages on the other. A clarification of the terminology employed in previous and current research on metalinguistic concepts, i.e. MLK and MLA, will be provided. Additionally, the chapter aims at disentangling the notion of attention from awareness, focusing on the cognitive aspect of the role played by MLA on additional language learning. Finally, it looks at the impact of different types of instruction settings on the development of MLA to highlight how language learning and MLA affect each other.

3.2 Defining Metalinguistic Awareness

But what is MLA and why is it considered of fundamental importance for the development of additional languages in bilinguals? To provide a general and commonly accepted definition of metalinguistic concepts is not an easy task. The labels used by academics to describe it may seem rather confusing due to the aforementioned different scientific approaches (i.e. cognitive, psychological, educational) adopted to analyse MLA and to the variety of competing terms employed to describe specific aspects of metalinguistic concepts. In Cenoz's (2003) view, MLA works as a mediator between bilingualism on the one hand and third (or additional) language acquisition on the other. This implies that bilingualism has a positive effect on the development of MLA and communicative skills and these factors, in turn, have an impact on the process of learning new languages. In other words, the positive effects of bilingualism on foreign language learning occur because they have a positive influence on MLA in the first place.

Following Malakoff's (1992) own definition, MLA:

> [a]llows the individual to step back from the comprehension or production of an utterance in order to consider the linguistic form and structure underlying the meaning of the utterance. Thus, a metalinguistic task is one which requires the individual to think about the linguistic nature of the message: to attend and to reflect on the structural features of the language. To be metalinguistically aware, then, is to know how to approach and solve certain types of problems which themselves demand certain cognitive and linguistic skills. (Malakoff, 1992: 518)

MLA can be considered a high-level cognitive ability that is part of the more general concept of metacognition. The *meta* prefix, in both metalinguistic and metacognition, is a Greek word that means beyond and entails going beyond language and cognition to call for an intentional, explicit and conscious ability. Metalinguistic refers to the consciousness or awareness of the linguistic aspects of a language. Similarly, metacognition 'is generally understood as the ability to contemplate one's own thinking, to observe oneself when processing cognitive tasks, and to organize the learning and thinking processes involved in these tasks' (Seel, 2012: 2228). Thus, metacognition involves the notion of awareness of one's cognitive processes that enables individuals to analyse and control the way they think and learn. By calling on metacognitive skills, performance skills are increased in a variety of situations where cognitive processes are involved.

An enormous contribution to a better understanding of the degree and nature of metalinguistic concepts comes from Bialystok's (2001) work *Bilingualism in Development*, where she managed to remarkably disambiguate the three main entities qualified by the term metalinguistic, i.e. knowledge, ability and awareness. In regard to the first concept, MLK (or knowledge about language), she states that what makes it different from knowledge about grammar is the level of generality at which rules are represented. 'It is the broader knowledge of abstract principles of languages which is distinct from the knowledge of a particular language'. On the other hand, the metalinguistic ability is portrayed as 'the capacity to use knowledge about language as opposed to the ability to use language' (2001: 124). According to Bialystok, this distinction makes it easy to explain why all children learn to speak but some of them struggle to acquire metalinguistic concepts. Moreover, it allows to further explain why MLA is the reserve of some privileged few, i.e. the more intelligent, the more educated, the more multilingual and so on. Finally, in order to have MLA, it is necessary that attention is actively focused on the domain of knowledge that describes the explicit properties of languages.

De Angelis (2007: 121), on the other hand, adopts the broader definition of MLA: 'the learners' ability to think of language and of perceiving language including the ability to separate meaning and forms, discriminate language components, identify ambiguity and understand the use of grammatical forms and structures'. It is worth noting that the author emphasises the importance of the role played by the formal context of acquisition of the languages involved in order to provide further MLK that learners can rely upon when learning additional languages. In other words, formal instruction in the L2 has been seen as a determining factor that has an impact on students' performance in an L3. What emerges from all the definitions taken into account is that MLA is both a cognitive and a linguistic factor that allows individuals to objectify language and better understand the working mechanisms beyond it. Thus, the development of MLA can be considered both a cause and an effect of language learning. On the one hand, it is improved through the formal instruction of languages since the conscious observation and manipulation of the linguistic elements are activated during the learning process. On the other hand, it is a fundamental resource that fosters the process and outcome of third or additional language acquisition since it enhances the understanding and use of language structures.

Hence, it can be argued that the reason why metalinguistic knowledge, ability and awareness have a positive influence on bilingual learners of additional languages is that they are all represented in an abstract and general sense so that they become explicit and universal and to be applied to any other language. Previous and current research in the field has resorted to a number of different arguments to explain the cause of the increased level of MLA reported in bilinguals which was also responsible for their better performance in the L3. Nonetheless, because of the complex nature of the relatively new field of study as well as the number of variables to consider in TLA, there is still no common agreement among scholars whether MLA is to be attributed mainly to the context of the acquisition of the L2 (i.e. formal/informal), the level of proficiency attained in the L2 or the amount of use and exposure to the language itself. Moreover, if it is commonly agreed among scholars that MLA is one of the first and most important variables that make bilinguals better language learners, it remains to be clarified whether MLA improves the process of language learning or whether it is the other way round.

Generally speaking, the most plausible explanation provided for bilinguals picking up languages faster and better than monolinguals takes into account two main factors, i.e. how the input is perceived and organised and how explicit knowledge relates to the speed of acquisition (Bowden *et al.*, 2005). The former deals with bilinguals' better processing strategies developed thanks to the process of adapting to the new language and the consecutive restructuring of their language system. Indeed, they use cognitive strategies that facilitate more efficient use of processing resources in the construction of formal rules. The latter assumes the weak interface position as a starting point. Indeed, explicit knowledge acts as an advanced organiser and focuses learners' attention on the relevant features of language. As a matter of fact, bilinguals show superior explicit knowledge of a target language. These benefits concern each level of the linguistic system: morphology, semantics and also syntactic and phonological awareness (Werker, 1986).

3.3 MLA and the Development of Multilingual Competence

The concept of MLA has been investigated from the point of view of its contribution to the development of multilingual competence. The concept of multilingual competence has been addressed by several scholars in the field of psycholinguistics (see Gabryś-Barker, 2019) in an attempt to portray the complexity and uniqueness of the multilingual mind. Cook (1991) was first to define the concept as the compound state of mind with two (three) grammars. Cenoz and Genesee (1998) describe multicompetence as an individual's ability to use several languages effectively. On the other hand, Aronin and O'Laoire (2001) conceive it as an ecosystem, underlining the state of constant change a multilingual person experiences due to the interaction of the various linguistic systems involved. An interesting discussion on the concept of multicompetence is provided by Gabryś-Barker (2019) after comparing and contrasting the most influential points of view in the literature. She observes that most of the experimental evidence supports the multicompetence model seen as holistic. Indeed, the mental lexicon of a multilingual demonstrates a close relationship between the first language (L1) and the L2/Ln. Phonological, lexical and syntactic processing in the L2/Ln are not separate and demonstrate relations and consultations between languages. This is again evidenced for example in users'/learners' code-switching between different languages.

So far, we have seen that the type of bilingualism, learner's proficiency, age of acquisition, linguistic domain, grammatical features and language typology may have an impact on the process and level of attainment in an L3. A further issue of paramount importance to consider is the linguistic background of the learner in relation to their literacy developed in the L2 and, specifically, their MLK. As defined by Jessner (2008b: 277), MLK is 'the ability to focus on linguistic form and to switch focus between form and meaning', and further that this knowledge is 'made up of a set of skills or abilities that the multilingual user develops owing to her/his prior linguistic and metacognitive knowledge' (Jessner, 2008b: 275).

The underlying assumption is that MLA is of crucial importance in TLA since it allows learners to consciously apply their existing knowledge of previously acquired languages, which, in Jessner's (2008b: 26) view, 'can contribute to the catalytic or accelerating effects in TLA'. Among the effects of language awareness mentioned by Knapp-Potthoff (1997: 11), it creates categories for the analysis and processing of the input, directs the focus on specific linguistic properties in the input, enables the application of appropriate language learning strategies and provides the basis for metacommunication. The importance of the development of MLA in the language education field has also been acknowledged by the *Common European Framework of Reference* (CEFR) for Languages as an essential element of the cognitive approach to multilingual learning and teaching.

> Plurilingual and pluricultural competence also promotes the development of linguistic and communication awareness, and even metacognitive strategies which enable the social agent to become more aware of and control his or her own 'spontaneous' ways of handling tasks and in particular their linguistic dimension. (Council of Europe, 2001: 134)

Indeed, the achievement of communicative competence in multiple languages is one of the main goals set by the European Commission, as reported in the *White Paper on Education and Training. Teaching and Learning. Towards the Learning Society* (European Commission, 1996: 67): 'it is becoming necessary to everyone, irrespective of training and education routes chosen, to be able to acquire and keep up their ability to communicate in at least two Community languages in addition to their mother tongue'. The European Commission thus highlights the importance of a particular aspect, communicative awareness, focused on the knowledge of how language functions, the communication strategies, the body language, etc. Nonetheless, MLA is a broader concept integrating language, communication and learning, including cognitive, affective, political and social parameters.

From a teaching and learning perspective, Hufeisen and Neuner (2003: 28) describe language learning awareness and linguistic awareness as crucial factors affecting the outcome of additional language acquisition strictly related to two aspects of language learning, i.e. declarative and procedural knowledge. The first refers to awareness and knowledge about language and enables the establishment of interlinguistic relations between the L1, L2 and the subsequent language. It is also on the basis of what is noticed and can be related to previous knowledge, as will be expanded on in the following sections. Procedural knowledge, on the other hand, includes awareness and knowledge about the foreign learning process and enables learners to consciously experience and reflect upon the process of language learning as well as on the type of learning strategies employed.

It has been argued that the beginning of a more intensive development of MLA, i.e. explicit knowledge of language, starts with formal instruction in the L1. For instance, insists on the importance of developing learners' and teachers' MLA, suggesting that more attention should be paid to the cognitive approach to learning, enhancing metacognition and metacommunication. However, this can only be accomplished by the implementation of 'awareness-raising techniques [...], enhancing the connections between languages in both teachers and learners; that is, bridging the languages, creating synergies and exploiting resources' (Jessner, 2008b: 38).

Given the multifaceted and complex nature of the phenomenon, it is not easy to characterise and measure MLA in both language acquisition and non-language acquisition domains such as cognitive psychology, cognitive science and neuroscience. Indeed, the role of awareness in learning is explicitly or implicitly subsumed into several variables in these fields, including type of learning, learning condition, type of awareness (i.e. language, metacognitive, conscious, unconscious) as well as constructs such as noticing and perception. Within the fields of study outside language acquisition, the concept of awareness has been vaguely defined. For instance, in cognitive psychology, Merikle *et al*. (2001: 116) make use of the term awareness as a synonym for consciousness when they point out that 'any evidence that perception is not necessarily accompanied by an awareness of perceiving attracts attention because it challenges the idea that perception implies consciousness'.

In second language acquisition (SLA) research, the most representative definition comes from Tomlin and Villa's (1994) work, where they point out that, generally speaking, awareness is a particular state of mind in which an individual has undergone a specific subjective experience of some cognitive context or external stimulus. The role of awareness in language learning is subsumed in many instruction or exposure strands of L2 research. Many studies consider the construct of awareness not as an independent variable but, instead, as an element which implicitly or explicitly plays a role in the processing of input in the noticing condition (e.g. Schmidt, 1990). More specifically, when dealing with language learning, these concepts are often associated with the term 'metalinguistic', i.e. MLA and MLK of the language.

The majority of the studies taken into account in the present work explain the instructed bilinguals' better performance in TLA in terms of higher MLA, improved linguistic strategies, communicative sensitivity, crosslinguistic awareness and sometimes even translation skills (e.g. Cenoz, 2003; Faerch & Kasper, 1983; James, 1996; Poulisse *et al.*, 1987). However, to the best of my knowledge, only a few studies directly compare these two types of bilingualism, i.e. instructed/uninstructed, based on the context of acquisition of the L2. Indeed, researchers generally compare monolinguals and bilinguals learning languages, while the effects of instruction or non-instruction in an L2 are usually overlooked or only marginally observed through post-studies regression analysis (Thomas, 1988).

As already argued, the general assumption that bilinguals are also better language learners has been supported by several studies which identified the enhanced level of MLA as the key element fostering the process of foreign language acquisition (e.g. Cenoz & Genesee, 1998; Jessner, 1999; Thomas, 1988). However, it is not entirely clear how and to what extent MLA helps multilingual learners to acquire an additional language. Investigating the role of previously known languages in L3 learning, Jaensch (2012) found that L3 German learners who began studying L2 English later in life (Japanese–English bilinguals) demonstrated a stronger ability to formulate new grammatical rules than learners who began L2 English learning at a younger age (Spanish–English bilinguals). A possible explanation put forward to account for this difference is that the more explicit English learning environment of the older learners resulted in enhanced MLA, in contrast to the more implicit learning environment of the younger learners. Cenoz (2001) found a similar effect when comparing learners aged 7–14, concluding that older children transferred more patterns from previously learned languages than younger children because older children have a greater awareness of linguistic similarity between two languages.

All in all, previous research suggests that both early and late bilingualism have potential benefits for subsequent language learning. On the one hand, early bilingualism is achieved in a more implicit language learning environment but gives learners access to two more-developed grammatical systems. Late bilingualism, on the other hand, is more explicit and facilitates the acquisition of formal rules in a subsequent language. While both accounts appeal to enhanced MLA, the route of acquisition of this awareness and the particular type of MLA under discussion appear to be distinct for early and late bilingualism. Accordingly, we expect that both early and late bilingualism lead to different types of advantages that are additive in nature: early bilinguals with additional formal L2 experience will receive further benefits beyond those of early bilingualism alone.

3.4 From Metalinguistic Knowledge to Metalinguistic Awareness

A particular aspect of MLA representing a controversial issue is whether it belongs to the linguistic or cognitive domain and whether it is a cause or an effect of cognitive and linguistic development. Again, this remains unclear because these develop through childhood and it is not always possible to separate them experimentally in children and relatively little research takes place on adults' MLA. Psycholinguists argue that the development of MLA is related to cognitive development because it involves cognitive processes that are different from those operating for language perception and production. Bialystok's (2001) interpretation to account for different findings from research into bilingualism and MLA, employing different tasks and looking at specific variables, concerns the difference between analysis and control. Following a comprehensive review of previous research into the effects of bilingualism and literacy, she concluded that higher levels of control increase with bilingualism, whereas higher levels of analysis increase with literacy. This accounts for different performances in different types of tasks for bilinguals with different linguistic and cognitive backgrounds. In particular, it has been observed that the advantage occurred most often when the level of bilingualism was controlled, i.e. balanced bilinguals performed better in all tasks.

Another possible interpretation provided by Bialystok (2001) accounts for the progression from MLK to MLA observed in the participants. This progression reflects an increase in the amount of attentional control required to accomplish tasks. Therefore, participants begin to show different results as soon as the task is aimed at assessing MLA rather than MLK. Yet, Rebuschat and Williams (2012) state that in psychology, the most commonly used criterion for discerning between implicit and explicit knowledge is the presence or lack of awareness. Implicit knowledge is unconscious knowledge that subjects are generally not aware of possessing whereas explicit knowledge is conscious knowledge that subjects are aware of possessing even though they may not always be able to provide an explanation for it.

The same view is shared by Robinson (2017), focusing on the role of attention as a measure to determine the aforementioned distinction between implicit and explicit learning. Attention and awareness are presented as two related concepts playing fundamental and different roles in the process of language learning. In particular, the two types of attention described are perceptual attention, which is automatic and involuntary, and focal attention, relying on some degree of voluntary executive control. As discussed, the issue of the amount and type of attention necessary to input in order for subsequent learning to occur, as well as the difference between noticing and understanding, has attracted much interest among academics in SLA (see Truscott & Sharwood Smith, 2011).

There is a wealth of literature on the role of attention in language learning (see Robinson *et al.*, 2012). One of the main features characterising this fundamental cognitive process is that it is limited and it is thought to be selective. In other words, only one attention-demanding processing task can be handled at a time. A further definitional aspect is that attention can be voluntary, meaning that it can be subject to control driven by the goals and intentions of the individual. In addition, attention is able to control access to consciousness. That is, under normal conditions, test takers can tell the researcher about their conscious perception, thoughts or feelings while performing a particular task. Specifically, voluntariness and consciousness are the features of attention that have been the object of intense debate since the quality of attention has been proved to affect language learning.

In cognitive and language acquisition domains, non-attentional learning means learning without focal attention to the input stimuli, selecting them for further processing and encoding in memory. It has been reported (Tomlin & Villa, 1994) that, in some cases, simple detection of input at a stage of perceptual processing prior to selection contributes to learning. In other words, learning could be said to take place without awareness since focal attention is widely acknowledged as a precondition for awareness. The focus has been put on learning under three attentional conditions: incidental (i.e. learning without intention, while doing something else), implicit (i.e. learning with no intervention of controlled attention, usually without providing rules and without asking to search for rules) and explicit (i.e. learning with the intervention of controlled attention).

Regarding the voluntariness of attention, the main question raised by researchers on language learning is whether or not it is possible to learn additional languages incidentally, as a consequence of doing something else. In SLA research, it is commonly agreed that incidental L2 learning is possible (Hulstijn, 2003; Krashen, 2004). Nonetheless, intentions fluctuate during online processing and it is online attention that is at stake in a cognitive understanding of L2 learning. In addition, it has been argued (Laufer & Hulstijn, 2001) that although learning without intention is possible, people learn faster, more and better when they deliberately apply themselves to the process of learning. Another controversial matter concerns learning without attention, that is whether it is possible to learn new language material just detected pre-attentively. More precisely, the question is whether detection is sufficient or noticing is a necessary requisite for additional language learning. The first is defined as a registration outside focal or selective attention (Tomlin & Villa, 1994), whereas noticing is defined as detection plus controlled activation into the focus of conscious attention (Schmidt, 1995). In particular, Schmidt (1994, 2001) has argued that detection which involves peripheral attention is not sufficient for learning since it cannot be codified in long-term memory. Instead, he maintains that 'what learners notice in input is what becomes intake for learning' (Schmidt, 1995: 20).

Interestingly, Nick Ellis (2002: 174) agrees with Schmidt's influential Noticing Hypothesis but only with the premises of the Implicit Tallying Hypothesis. In other words, first, noticing is necessary only for new elements with certain properties making low-attentional learning unlikely but not for all aspects of language. Second, noticing may only be necessary for the initial registration of such difficult elements but not for subsequent encounters. Schmidt (2001) modified his initial claim, acknowledging that it may be impossible to empirically record zero noticing at the time of processing. Since then, he has maintained that 'more noticing leads to more learning' (Schmidt, 1994: 18), suggesting that it may enhance and facilitate the process of language learning.

Regarding the role of attention and noticing in TLA, to the best of my knowledge, no studies are available in the literature specifically dealing with multilingual learning. Based on the discussed sources, it can be inferred that if conscious attention on the formal aspects of a language is required for L2 learning to occur, the same outcomes should be expected in additional language learning too. However, to test this hypothesis, further research is needed, including multilingual participants with different modes of instruction of L2/L3/Ln.

3.5 Implicit and Explicit Metalinguistic Awareness and Language Learning

It is important to note that the Noticing Hypothesis assumes that 'learning requires awareness at the time of learning' (Schmidt, 1995: 26). That is, it does not posit that learners need to remain aware of what they have noticed afterwards. Also, learners' noticing does not necessarily imply that what they have noticed has been understood. The predictions of the Noticing Hypothesis have been tested on the basis of the presence or absence of self-reported, retrospective awareness. Thus, another controversial issue, difficult to observe and record experimentally, concerns the dissociation between attention and awareness. In other words, whether or not new linguistic material can be learned without awareness. However, it has been widely acknowledged that demonstrating the presence or lack of awareness at the time of learning is extremely difficult. Introspective and retrospective self-reports can be considered imperfect and insufficient methods.

A number of scholars in the field of language acquisition have been interested in the process and outcome of learning without the focus of explicit, declarative information of what has been learned (Rebuschat,

2015), i.e. the process of implicit learning without focusing on rules. More specifically, the question of interest is whether grammar generalisation can result from processing the linguistic input without explicit knowledge. At this point, the question of interest is whether implicit learning can lead to the development of implicit MLA. As Kemp (2001) points out, MLA can be implicit, explicit or at an intermediate stage on the continuum. Nonetheless, implicit MLA is extremely difficult to observe experimentally and, due to its inaccessibility, it is also difficult to test and record. The majority of tests focused on awareness of grammatical form employ artificial grammars of meaningless strings of letters based on strict sets of rules. After a learning condition, a testing condition usually follows, presenting the stimuli produced from the same grammar but which have not been presented to the test takers. In this way, participants are tested not only on their ability to memorise sets of strings but also on their ability to make grammatical inferences.

For instance, a recent work by D'Angelo and Sorace (2022) tested the assumption that formal instruction in multiple languages enhances MLA in bilinguals which, in turn, facilitates the process of TLA. The participants, 42 bilinguals with different levels of proficiency and MLA developed in German L2, were assessed on their ability to learn an additional language through an artificial language task (Llama-F; Meara, 2005). The main aim of the study was to examine the relationship between bilinguals' level of explicit MLA and their performance on the TLA task. The influence of various potential predictors was considered, including explicit MLA, number of languages mastered, overall proficiency and amount of instruction received in German L2. The results indicated that bilinguals with higher levels of explicit MLA also performed better in TLA, after controlling for the aforementioned variables in the model. The findings suggest that, to observe a positive outcome in additional languages, learners should be stimulated and assisted in the process of conscious reflection and manipulation of the language system(s) as well as of the learning strategies developed in previous languages.

Nonetheless, the validity of artificial language tests has been questioned since, according to some scholars, it is not possible to test implicit awareness of grammatical form without testing the understanding of meaning. Despite the acknowledged importance of artificial language learning (ALL) experiments as tools exploring the principles of language, as well as language learning ability, a persistent question is whether ALL studies can be considered ecologically valid assessments of natural language ability. Indeed, it has been argued (Schmidt, 1994) that learning artificial languages differs from learning natural languages under different points of view. First, artificial grammars are meaningless whereas natural languages are mainly based on communicating meaning. Second, in terms of time of learning, ALL takes place over a limited range of time, set by the researcher. On the other hand, natural language learning occurs over a long period of time. In regard to the syntactic structure, in natural language learning, the position of each element affects the whole structure, differently from the artificial language where the letter order only constitutes a spatial pattern. Moreover, what differs between the two processes is that natural language learners do not usually receive instruction merely based on searching for rules and memorisation. Nonetheless, both natural languages and artificial grammars have been considered as 'a product of a complex underlying system' (Schmidt, 1994: 167).

Several studies assessed the validity of artificial language tasks by comparing their performance with that recorded in natural language tasks, controlling for a number of internal factors (Robinson, 2011). Ettlinger *et al.* (2015), for instance, bridged the gap between ALL and natural language learning research by comparing the performance of adult learners of Spanish as an L2 and ALL enhancement. The findings suggest that performance on ALL tasks positively correlates with indices of L2 learning even after controlling for IQ, general intelligence and the potential mediation of the internal factors. The authors also considered the effects of specific features of ALL tasks such as including or not a semantic aspect as well as presenting a complex or simple grammar. Interestingly enough, they inferred that ALL studies that incorporate a semantic component and involve more complicated grammatical systems may closely resemble the learning process of natural languages.

3.6 The Role of Language Use and Language Knowledge in Third Language Acquisition

Further evidence to better understand the role of MLA under the specific circumstances of language learning comes from Bialystok and Barac's (2012) work. In their study, they provide an accurate analysis of the different factors associated with the reported advantages found in fully bilinguals in order to dissociate the effects of MLA and executive control. More specifically, the research aim was to identify the specific features of the bilingual experience responsible for the different performance on metalinguistic and executive function tasks in emergent bilingual children. The results demonstrated that the two areas investigated are affected by different aspects of bilingualism. That is, metalinguistic performance improved with increasing knowledge of the language of testing whereas performance in executive control tasks improved with more experience in a bilingual education environment. This dissociation has a great impact on previous research into bilingualism for at least three main reasons. First, these findings highlight the importance of being exposed to multiple languages in educational settings in order to improve children's executive functions. Moreover, an important implication of the study is that it questions previous research assumptions that fully balanced bilingualism is a necessary condition for modifications in executive functioning to occur (e.g. Bialystok & Majumder, 1998; Carlson & Meltzoff, 2008). Instead, the study shows that the accumulation of experience in a formal bilingual setting also contributes to the development of executive control in those children.

In addition, the results obtained support the view that MLA and literacy foster the process and outcome of additional language acquisition, contributing to shed light on the role of language use and language knowledge in TLA. A previous study by Mägiste (1984, 1986), for example, suggested that differences in performance were to be attributed to whether a language was used or not rather than to the level of literacy achieved in the L2 (Mägiste, 1984, 1986). This pattern was evident with different types of tests administered. The popular view in the literature that people who become bilingual at an early stage will later have greater facility in picking up an L3 is only partially acknowledged by the author. Indeed, she states that if, on the one hand, this is certainly the case at certain metalinguistic levels, on the other, it does not occur automatically at a very elementary level of language learning, where it seems to be more a question of strategy.

Another important implication of Bialystok and Barac's (2012) study is that it helps to clarify the relationship between metalinguistic performance and bilingualism, providing evidence to promote the formal study of languages too. Indeed, unlike executive control, metalinguistic advantages have been observed even in participants with lower levels of bilingualism. Therefore, it can be argued that what makes the difference in metalinguistic tasks is not the degree of bilingualism but the level of linguistic proficiency attained in that language. Indeed, knowledge of English was associated with higher metalinguistic performance in English but this relationship would be expected in monolingual children too. What was surprising is that an increased level of bilingualism was not necessarily associated with enhanced performance in the task. According to the authors, this could be explained by the fact that bilingualism helps to develop and understand structural relations within languages; however, beyond that insight, more bilingual experience does not lead to further development in that area. Finally, what makes the study particularly relevant and worth mentioning is the contribution it makes to understanding the mechanism by which bilingualism affects cognitive and linguistic outcomes by taking into account two aspects of bilingualism responsible for differences between monolinguals and bilinguals, i.e. proficiency and use.

Indeed, the outcomes of bilingualism depend on both the achievement of adequate linguistic proficiency and experience using two languages. These factors can be explained in terms of the previously mentioned distinction, advanced by Bialystok, between the representational structure of knowledge and control of attention. In particular, metalinguistic tasks focus on linguistic representations and representational structure is sensitive to increasing knowledge. In other words, knowing two languages improves the knowledge of abstract linguistic structures and, therefore, bilingualism fosters metalinguistic performance. However, it is the absolute level of linguistic knowledge and not the degree of bilingualism that plays a role in TLA development. On the other hand, control of attention is sensitive to accumulating experience and performance in executive control tasks depends on domain-general systems also involved in bilingual language processing. However, a certain amount of time is required for these systems to reach a certain level that allows them to influence non-linguistic domains. Therefore, it can be claimed that the two main areas where a positive bilingual effect has been observed, i.e. MLA and executive control, are influenced by different kinds of experiences: the achievement of adequate linguistic proficiency for the former and accumulated practice in the language for the latter.

3.7 Other Factors Affecting the Development of Metalinguistic Awareness: Schooling and Literacy

An ongoing debate in the field of cognitive linguistics concerns the relationship between literacy and MLA. Is it MLA that enhances the development of literacy or is it the other way round? There are studies supporting the view that MLA functions as a facilitator in the initial stage of literacy development (Kemp, 2001). However, other studies (e.g. Olson, 1991) maintain that MLA is a product of literacy. Nowadays, there is ample support to claim that MLA can be considered as both a requisite and a consequence of literacy learning. By turning language into a visual medium, the focus of languages is not just on speaking and listening but also on writing and reading, which makes languages objects to manipulate and consciously analyse. Moreover, it has been argued that apart from focusing on form, writing involves a number of other fundamental aspects, different from spoken language. Among the features mentioned by Coulmas (1989), three of them specifically contribute to the development of MLA, i.e. reifying function, mnemonic function and aesthetic function. The reifying function, in particular, makes language visible and analysable with regard to its grammatical structure. As Olson (1991: 266) states, 'Learning to read and write significantly increases MLA because fixed written text that is available for rescanning, comparison, commentary and analysis promotes the objectification of language'.

On the other hand, research on the role of MLA in emerging literacy has established that metalinguistic abilities at the phonological, syntactic, print and pragmatic levels are linked to later literacy achievements. An interesting study (Lazo *et al.*, 1997) has examined the interplay among these skills and developing reading and spelling skills. Specifically, the authors used time-reversed path analyses to test the hypothesis that MLA registers stronger and direct effects on literacy than early pre-conventional reading and invented spelling skills. The study was conducted on 60 children aged 54 months with measures of metalinguistic abilities, pre-conventional reading and invented spelling. Results showed that pre-conventional reading and invented spelling influenced each other across the development and had stronger direct effects on subsequent literacy than did aspects of MLA. On the other hand, pre-literate metalinguistic abilities were shown to affect pre-conventional reading and invented spelling skills and combine with these to influence further growth in literacy.

On the relationship between MLA development and literacy, it is worth discussing a recent work by Trybulec (2021) where the author integrates two different perspectives on MLA: the metacognitive theory of writing (MTW) and the distributed language perspective (DLP). Although the aforementioned approaches converge on many points, they seem to disagree about the status of MLA and its sources of development. For both, MLA represents an intrinsic property of first-order languaging, i.e. meaning-making and building knowledge by means of language. Harris (1998: 20) maintains that 'all human beings engage in analytic reflection about their own linguistic experience: this is a sine qua non of engaging in language itself'. However, the MTW emphasises the role of literacy, suggesting that 'language becomes something to talk about primarily in literate contexts, book reading, learning to read and write and talking about what is read' (Olson, 2016: 71–72). In other words, literacy is considered an additional support to make languages visible in order to facilitate the analytical thinking about language structures.

The MTW argues that manipulations of aggregates of written symbolisations activate layers of MLK (i.e. phonemic, lexical, semantic) which are otherwise unavailable. Training in reading and writing leads children to develop standards for judging the identity of linguistic repetition. Nonetheless, repetition is also possible in oral cultures and among pre-reading children. Indeed, pre-reading children display a high level of phonetic sensitivity, including imitating and memorising simple and complex vocalisations, recognising rhymes and rhythms and spotting anomalies in the speech of their caregivers. Thus, the basic difference between the MTW and integrationists/DLP concerns the status and sources of MLA. Olson considers MLA to be an exclusive property of the literate mind while integrationists/DLP stress that MLA is inherently inscribed in the daily practices of languaging displayed in such mundane linguistic activities as asking for repetition, naming practices or learning a ritual formula in an oral culture. Olson (2016: 113) highlights that 'learning a language is a universal human achievement, thinking about language is a product of and fostered by literacy'. In contrast, integrationists maintain that MLA is, in fact, universal.

This psychological and philosophical theorising about metacognition, which is closely related to the issue of MLA, allows broad pluralism towards the types of awareness. The distinction between procedural and analytical awareness should not be perceived as a dichotomy. Instead, they should be conceived as 'the extremes of the continuum spanning from tacit and minimal awareness with the low level of attention control and virtually no distance to its object, to advanced forms of deliberately guided selective attention with full-blown ability to "distance" oneself from the flow of language' (Trybulec, 2021: 10). Hence, taking into account the point of view conveyed by Olson (2016), it can be argued that in additional language learning, where the sources of input are multiple, MLA and literacy become even more important. They play a crucial role supporting the analysis, meaning making and knowledge building, resorting to literacy developed in any previous language mastered.

3.8 Strategies to Develop Metalinguistic Awareness

As already argued, MLA is the ability to analyse, to talk and to think about language as an object, independently of the concrete meaning of each word. Metalinguistic skills, on the other hand, allow people to observe and control their use of language. MLA has also been conceived as 'a type of metacognition' (Varga, 2021), the ability to regard language as a code and distinguish it from its symbolic meaning. Hence, it follows that MLA skills can be a strong predictor of language development and ability to learn new languages in that they help to understand language and its structure.

To promote the development of metacognition, it is advisable to use metacognitive strategies, such as planning, self-assessment and self-regulation. When applied to language, these strategies contribute to enhancing MLA. Since this development is not limited to a specific age range, it should be promoted at all learning levels. Moreover, the majority of educational activities employed nowadays are suitable for young learners since they are mainly used in school contexts (e.g. Roth *et al.*, 1996; Zipke, 2008). Several studies (e.g. Bloor, 1986; El Euch, 2010, 2011) have shown a very low level of MLA in undergraduate students and have related this level to the students' low performance level in tests that call for analytic and argumentative skills. Hence, this section is focused on the strategies developed to enhance the level of MLA of adult L3/Ln learners.

3.8.1 Self-talk

An essential strategy identified to develop metacognition is self-talk. Educators and teachers usually employ this strategy in their problem-solving process to make sure their actions are well understood and to improve their classroom management skills. Most importantly, self-talk should be encouraged in learners as part of their learning development. It contributes to developing awareness of what is expected and understood in a text, both oral and written, to make sure that the message has been clearly internalised by the learners. For instance, when dealing with fuzzy or ambiguous messages, learners can be trained to make the message clearer and more explicit through self-talk. Later, they will transfer this strategy to their own messages in the process of producing them whether orally or in writing. By thinking about the language used in a text, learners can develop an awareness of the different parts of speech to make the message more explicit. Self-talk leads to a continuous analysis of the language used (Gabryś-Barker, 2012).

3.8.2 Predicting

A further strategy that contributes to the enhancement of MLA is predicting or making hypotheses relying on what is already known to guess missing information. Indeed, trying to figure out which is the correct guess or prediction involves a good analysis of the available information and a sense of logic to understand which piece of information is missing. Moreover, it activates background knowledge, draws attention to the main concepts and words and encourages learners to go beyond the surface and figure out concepts and things. In a second phase, learners are usually asked to read or listen to the text to make sure they made the correct predictions. This process of predicting and revising assists students in thinking, analysing and making deep sense of the message at hand. In case of incorrect predictions, students are required to refer to and incorporate new elements to adjust their thinking accordingly, creating new connections. A number of predicting activities have been identified and listed by El Euch and Huot (2015). According to the authors, it is advisable to adapt them to the learners' level and to the context of learning. Most importantly, when targeting the development of MLA, these activities need to be followed by a justification to make sure students make their thoughts explicit.

- Predicting the meaning of unknown words from surrounding text.
- Predicting the meaning of a sentence whose structure is unknown or complex.
- Predicting a conclusion, based on previous parts of the text.
- Predicting a decision based on pros and cons.
- Predicting an opinion based on for and against arguments.

3.8.3 Paraphrasing

Paraphrasing is the comprehension and production of another person's oral or written text. It involves, first of all, a thorough understanding of the message, i.e. analysing the words and sentences to make sense of them. Secondly, it requires the employment of different sentences and words to convey the same ideas. Hence, paraphrasing calls for two fundamental cognitive processes already discussed in this chapter, i.e. language analysis and language control. Paraphrasing activities may involve different levels of linguistic analysis. For example, asking students to provide synonyms, to change the sentence from active to passive voice, to combine or separate sentences or to convey the meaning of a whole paragraph in their own words.

On the role of paraphrasing in the development of MLA, it is worth recalling the importance of translation for adult bilinguals dealing with additional languages. Indeed, translation has been defined as 'interlanguage paraphrase' or 'intralanguage translation' (Malakoff & Hakuta, 1991). In both, the objective is to take a piece of information and recode the meaning in a different linguistic form. In translation the form is a different language whereas in paraphrasing the form needs to be found within the same language (Fuchs, 1982). Hence, translation and paraphrasing can both be considered fundamental tasks improving MLA in that they both depend on the ability to extract meaning from an utterance, to understand and reproduce the equivalent meaning in another utterance. However, the vocabulary demands of the two tasks differ in that paraphrasing requires a large vocabulary within the same language, while translation requires only a basic vocabulary in each of two languages.

3.8.4 Summarising

Summarising is another strategy suggested by El Euch and Huot (2015). School principals and teachers often use the summarising strategy to focus attention on the main contents expressed in a meeting or a lesson. Students should be trained to use this strategy efficiently. The authors suggest two specific activities to improve this skill.

- Activity 1: Students are asked to (1) highlight (or underline) the parts of the text that need to be focused on; (2) write a text with the highlighted (or underlined) parts; (3) in pairs, students exchange their texts and discuss/justify their choice of the parts of speech they selected from the original text.
- Activity 2: Students are asked to (1) keep a journal for courses; (2) in pairs, they discuss the correctness and the pertinence of the information kept in their respective journals. (El Euch & Huot, 2015: 7)

This technique is effective in the development of MLA for a number of reasons. First, summarising allows learners to keep their attention focused on the selected aspects of the text, enhancing the receptive comprehension skills. Moreover, it implies reusing the selected linguistic elements in context, in the discussion phase, fostering both the written and oral production skills.

3.8.5 Comparing sentences with discourse markers and coherence relations

Coherence relations are relations in discourse that join sentences or clauses to express cause, condition, elaboration, justification or evidence. Discourse markers (e.g. but, because, then, already) are essential to guide the reader or listener in the recognition of these types of relations. The task of comparing sentences with discourse markers and coherence relations fosters learners' MLA in both sentences. Comparing and contrasting sentences improves the students' language control ability. A comparison task has been included in several MLA tests (e.g. Pinto & El Euch, 2015) to assess the level of MLA developed in the comprehension of different types of relations (i.e. qualitative, temporal and spatiotemporal). For example, in the test developed by Pinto *et al.* (1999), students were asked to indicate whether each pair of the following sentences deals with the same type of quality and to justify their answers:

(1) He provided an acceptable solution to the problem. – He provided a good solution to the problem.
(2) Read first, then think. – Start thinking after reading.
(3) The city hall is facing the theatre. – The theatre is facing the city hall.

On the other hand, Roehr's (2008) test of MLA was developed to incorporate measures of L2 proficiency on the one hand, and language analytic abilities on the other. She found that the linguistic and metalinguistic knowledge of advanced university-level L1 English learners of L2 German correlated strongly. Moreover, the study suggests that learners' ability to correct, describe and explain highlighted L2 errors and their L2 language analytic ability may constitute components of the same construct. The test is worth mentioning since it allows to distinguish among three levels of MLA, that is three levels of explicitness of grammatical knowledge of German L2. In particular, the construct of L2 MLK was operationalised by means of a two-section test. The first section was aimed at measuring learners' ability to correct, describe and explain selected L2 features. The second section was aimed at measuring learners' language analytic ability.

Items targeting the syntactic, morphological and lexical features of the L2 were included. Roehr's language test involves a range of L2 features representative of aspects covered in tertiary-level foreign language instruction for L1 English-speaking learners of L2 German. Therefore, targeted features were based on notions of pedagogical grammar (McDonough, 2002; Westney & Odlin, 1994), rather than a specific linguistic theory. In accordance with this rationale, the explicit MLA test includes:

- features of the L2 constituting either real cognates, in the sense that direct;
- English translation equivalents exist (e.g. modal particles), or false cognates, in the sense that apparent analogies between the L1 and L2 mask formal or functional differences (e.g. German *seit* typically combining with the present tense as opposed to English *since* typically combining with the present perfect tense);
- functional features of the L2 that exist in English but differ in terms of their formal realisations (e.g. word order in subordinate clauses; passive constructions); and formal features of the L2 that have no direct equivalents in English (e.g. separable verbs; grammatical gender).

What is worth discussing in more detail about this test of MLA is that it provides a valid instrument to portray the MLA level of additional language learners developed in an L2. This allows us to make inferences on the facilitative role of MLA in additional languages in that the elements that have been observed and analysed in the L2 are likely to be used during the process of TLA. Indeed, it must be borne in mind that the mediating role of MLA in TLA is due to conceiving the language as an abstract system, made of different levels, interacting among each other. In other words, MLA enhances the process and outcomes of additional language learning in that it does not need to be referred to any specific language but it can be applied to the analytical and inferring processes involved when dealing with other languages.

3.9 Learning Strategies and Cognitive Development

As discussed, not only do learning strategies facilitate additional language learning, but they also foster proficiency and contribute to the cognitive development of experienced language learners (Jessner, 2006; McLaughlin, 1990). Different studies in SLA and TLA support these assumptions confirming that 'the number of language learning strategies available to a learner was dependent on prior linguistic experience and the proficiency levels in the individual languages' (Jessner, 2006: 127). Nonetheless, if, on the one hand, strategic processing in (predominantly) bilinguals is a widely researched area, on the other, strategic processing within highly experienced multilinguals still represents an overlooked field that needs to be better explored. Whereas there are a number of studies comparing bilinguals' and monolinguals' application of language learning strategies to additional language learning, there is little research comparing monolinguals' and multilinguals' language learning strategic processing (Török & Jessner, 2017).

Dahm's (2015) study represents one of the most recent works investigating the strategies developed by experienced multilingual language learners. The author reports a strategy study, carried out as part of a large-scale classroom investigation within Pluralistic Approach to Unknown Languages (PAUL) sessions, in which students were confronted with three unknown languages: Dutch, Italian and Finnish. The three sessions were carried out consecutively and based on metasemantic, metasyntactic and metaphonological tasks. The results of the study showed that multilingual strategy training influences the use of speakers' strategies. Interestingly, the study reveals that the perceived linguistic distance between the multilinguals' source and the target language does play a role in the choice of strategy employed. Additionally, there was also a further difference in the application of the different strategies. That is, comparison and translation were the most utilised strategies while inferencing was the least utilised. The results contribute to a better understanding of crosslinguistic interaction in TLA involving the implementation of metalinguistic and metacognitive strategies in TLA. Thus, they emphasise the demand for implementing strategy training into language teaching classes (see Jessner et al., 2016).

A study by O'Laoire (2001) investigated the strategy use of Irish learners of German and French. The findings showed how the English/Irish bilinguals made more use of strategies than the learners who were dominant in English. Interestingly, the same study repeated three years later on the same population revealed that the MLA associated with bilinguals learners of TLA in the study of Irish was considerable even in the context of underachievement (O'Laoire, 2004). An additional step forward to a thorough understanding of language strategies comes from a large-scale study by Mißler (1999). Employing a German version of the Strategy Inventory for Language Learning (SILL), Oxford (1990) revealed that strategy use of multilinguals depended on individual factors, and that the quantity of the strategies used increased with the novel language learning experience. This was further confirmed and clarified by Müller-Lancé (2003a, 2003b), who developed a strategy model of multilingual learning. The focus was on the monitoring function within inferencing processes, which directly affects the success of strategies.

In a study conducted in 2006, Jessner demonstrated the simultaneous activation of the languages in a multilingual learner's repertoire while searching for words in TLA. Her work confirmed the findings of a study by Kellerman and Bialystok (1997), who highlighted how multilinguals apply communication strategies associated with the aforementioned metalinguistic aspects of control and analysis. Monitoring functions such as detection and error correction are included in these processes and, in case of linguistic discrepancy, these two processes become unbalanced. That is why multilingual learners have been reported to make use of strategies to repair errors in communication, either consciously or unconsciously (Faerch & Kasper, 1983).

Another interesting work on strategic processing in multilinguals was carried out by Kemp (2007). She investigated the way 144 bilingual and multilingual foreign language learners applied grammar learning strategies to additional language learning. The number of languages of the participants varied between two and 12, including indigenous, foreign, heritage and classical languages. The results demonstrated that the number of languages a multilingual foreign language learner knew strongly correlates with the quantity and frequency of the applied grammar strategies. This was also confirmed by the learning strategies that participants themselves reported using. Interestingly enough, Kemp also found that this growing trend was particularly frequent when the number of languages was more than three.

Regarding strategy use and application, the findings of the longitudinal Linguistic Awareness in Language Attriters (LAILA) study carried out in Tyrol showed that the application of multilingual compensatory strategies revealed a close relationship between crosslinguistic interaction and linguistic awareness (see Jessner et al., 2016). Beginning in March 2011 and ending in February 2016, the project investigated the development of MLA in foreign language knowledge and its importance connected to language attrition. The participants of the study applied various types of strategic processing: German-based and Italian-based strategies and strategies in which the subjects used both of these languages in order to find the right word in English. Regarding their function, strategies to compensate for lexical insecurity or a complete deficiency in the target language were used alongside compensatory strategies applied in order to find lexical alternatives. Simplification, facilitation and avoidance strategies were also detected as part of the strategic processing.

3.10 Conclusion

To conclude, after comparing and contrasting previous and current research focused on specific aspects of the relationship between the level of MLA developed, previous language learning experience and TLA, it can be argued that there are at least two main aspects that still need to be further explored. That is, in order to have a broader understanding of the role played by MLA in additional language learning as well as a common agreement in the field of research, task construal and sensitivity of measurement of awareness need to be considered as crucial factors in future studies. Accordingly, it would be worth adopting sensitive measures to detect the status of awareness under different points of view, i.e. cognitive, psychological and linguistic on the one hand and new methodologies to operationalise these fundamental aspects of language learning on the other. Additionally, the context of acquisition of bilinguals' L2 should be considered as a separate individual difference variable which affects the process and outcome of language learning for two main reasons. First, on the basis of the evidence provided by the most influential works taken into account, it can be suggested that it plays a crucial role in the development of more effective learning strategies and enhanced MLA. Second, in order to observe the positive effects of bilingualism on the acquisition of third or additional languages in a formal environment, it is necessary that bilingualism is supported by instruction in both L1 and L2.

Thus, across all the studies reviewed, it is possible to conclude that despite the considerable interest among scholars in the relatively new field, there is still a lot to investigate due to the high complexity of the phenomenon. The numerous variables involved that need to be controlled at the same time, such as age of acquisition, context of acquisition, level of proficiency and typological proximity of at least three different languages involved, together with the difficulty in measuring and determining what is implicit and explicit, make TLA a complex phenomenon to study. Indeed, the expectation that research into the psychological, linguistic and cognitive consequences of bilingualism should produce completely consistent results is a false premise. In other words, there is not one single phenomenon called bilingualism which ought to influence the mental lives of all bilinguals in the same way. Accordingly, research should be directed towards identifying those conditions under which bilingual learning experiences are likely to enhance or delay all the different aspects of cognitive growth, with the context of acquisition of previous languages one of the most important.

Among the different factors affecting TLA, based on the results observed and discussed in the selected studies, it can be argued that MLA does play a crucial, mediating role in additional language learning. Indeed, this fundamental skill, included in the metacognitive abilities, supports and facilitates the process of TLA by turning the language into a visual object and enhancing the analytic mechanism of inferring and meaning making across all the languages involved in the multilingual repertoire. Nonetheless, it is important to bear in mind that one cannot separate the effects of MLA from all the other internal and external factors involved in the process of language learning. By explicitly focusing attention on the internal structure of languages, formal instruction, in particular, contributes to enhancing MLA by turning the language into a visual object to manipulate and analyse. This explains the better performance observed in bilingual learners of an L3/Ln who had also learned the L2 in a formal context compared to those bilinguals who only received instruction in the L1.

4 Multilingual Education and Translanguaging: A 'Practical Theory of Languages'

4.1 Introduction

Approaches to multilingualism and multilingual education differ considerably in terms of how multilingualism is conceived and the way languages in the multilingual speaker and learner of additional languages are construed. On the one hand, scholars from the formal approach maintain that languages are clearly circumscribed and transferable identities (González-Alonso *et al.*, 2017; Puig-Mayenco *et al.*, 2018). On the other hand, supporters of the Dynamic System Theory (Herdina & Jessner, 2002) put forward the view that languages are dynamically integrated subsystems. The most interesting approach, in terms of the countability and delimitation of language varieties, comes from an innovative pedagogical theory and practice, particularly suitable for the context of multilingual acquisition, i.e. translanguaging (García & Li, 2014).

This chapter discusses the way translanguaging can be conceived as a linguistic theory going beyond the countability of languages. These are conceived as unbounded, fluid and interwoven systems. The work describes and analyses different social contexts where translanguaging is particularly advisable to enhance the multilingual repertoire of learners coming from diverse linguistic, cognitive and sociocultural backgrounds. Additionally, it suggests implementing translanguaging techniques and strategies aimed at developing the metalinguistic awareness (MLA) of languages and preserving minority and heritage languages (HLs) and identities. Additionally, it discusses the theoretical debate dividing translanguage theorists on the legitimacy of code-switching and additive bilingualism.

4.2 Multilingual Repertoire: Soft Boundaries between Linguistic Systems

Different from second language acquisition (SLA), the main focus of studies on third language acquisition (TLA) has been the multilingual learners' unique cognitive profile and linguistic repertoire including multiple varieties of languages, with different levels of proficiency and registers mastered, acquired in diverse educational contexts and social realities contributing to the perceived prestige of those languages as well as the attitude towards them. In other words, the shift here is from an ideal monolingual learner to real learners of additional languages.

The translanguaging approach to multilingual education allows us to encompass the categorical dichotomies from the past between monolinguals and bilinguals, propounding innovative aspects in terms of linguistic theories and pedagogical approaches to multilingualism. First of all, referring to *trans-system* and *trans-space* means being focused on students' subjectivity, enabling the engagement of multiple meaning-making systems through a fluid practice going beyond and between different language education systems, structures and practices. Second, its *transformative* nature has been seen as a new configuration of language and education where old concepts and structures are surpassed with the goal of transforming learners' subjectivities, identities, cognitive and social structures. Regarding the impact on the language and education analysis, a *transdisciplinary* approach provides a lens through which a broader understanding of human sociality, human cognition and human learning is possible (García & Li, 2015).

Hence, translanguaging is used as an umbrella term including a wide variety of examples of both theories and practices of the fluid use of languages, breaking the traditional conventions and the strict purist ideologies in order to get closer to the way people communicate in their everyday lives. An interesting work by Li Wei (2018) is centred upon the main reasons why translanguaging meets the need of a practical theory of language in applied linguistics. He states that his main concern is not to identify and define different instances of translanguaging; instead, the author recognises the need for an innovative approach to multilingualism that suits the complex linguistic realities of the 21st century. Despite the acknowledgement of multilingualism as a reality of having different languages coexisting in different parts of the world, what still remains problematic, nowadays, is the mixing of languages. Indeed, the author points out that one of the most important post-multilingualism challenges concerns the recognition of multiple and complex interweavings of languages and linguistic varieties, where boundaries between languages and other semiotic means are constantly reassessed and adjusted. Following this line, concepts such as indigenous, native and minority language are questioned.

What is worth recalling about Li Wei's own reconceptualisation of translanguaging, as both practice and process, is the cognitive added value of the concept:

> By adding the trans prefix to languaging, I not only wanted to have a term that better captures multilingual language users' fluid and dynamic

practices [...] but also put forward two further arguments: 1. Multilinguals do not think unilingually in a politically named linguistic entity, even when they are in a monolingual mode and producing one nameable language only for a specific stretch of speech or text. 2. Human beings think beyond language, and thinking requires the use of a variety of cognitive, semiotic, and modal resources of which language in its conventional sense of speech and writing is only one. (Li, 2018: 18)

What Li Wei highlights in the passage is the interrelation of language processing with other auditory and visual processes. Like any other cognitive process, it cannot be considered as independent and, what is more, the language experience of multilingual learners and users is closely interconnected and mutually beneficial. Language being a multisensory and multimodal semiotic system, interconnected with all the other cognitive systems, for the author translanguaging means overcoming the separation between linguistic, non-linguistic, semiotic and cognitive systems.

One of the most interesting assumptions supported by translanguaging theories is the existence of a multilingual repertoire which differs considerably from the monolingual native speaker. As a matter of fact, multilingual learners need to speak different languages to serve a variety of functions. Therefore, having an idealised monolingual native speaker as a point of reference for each language mastered is far from a possible reality. Not only do multilingual learners acquire new linguistic and semiotic skills when dealing with additional languages but, most importantly, they reconstruct and adjust their repertoire to accommodate other languages. The features that the new language may have in common with the learners' linguistic background refer not only to the grammatical aspects of the language but also to the emotional dimension affecting the learning process such as aptitude and motivation (see Chapter 2).

The construal of the multilingual repertoire constitutes an enlightening example of a linguistic theory which questions the countability and delimitations among languages. The expression 'languaging' refers to an approach to languages that is more focused on the individuals' contextualised social activities rather than languages conceived as abstract systems. In Pennycook's (2010: 2) words, 'to look at language as a practice is to view language as an activity rather than a structure, as something we do rather than a system we draw on, as material part of social and cultural life rather than an abstract identity'.

Suggesting a translanguaging approach to multilingualism, García and Li (2014) overcome the ideal of languages as independent systems and the interdependence view assuming some degrees of mutual influence. Indeed, taking some concepts from the fields of sociolinguistics and psycholinguistics, their notion of translanguaging conceives the linguistic repertoire not as composed of systems or subsystems but as a unified identity with a set of linguistic features. That is, their Dynamic Bilingual

Model, related to their theories on translanguaging, 'posits that there is but one linguistic system [...] with features that are integrated throughout' (García & Li, 2014: 15).

It is crucial to clarify that here the term 'system' has a particular meaning in that the focus is on using languages rather than conceiving them as static entities made of different sublevels. According to the authors, languages only exist as social constructions, they simply become specific patterns of a selection of linguistic features in the repertoire. The latter is different from the concept of communicative competence to be reached in SLA. Although communicative competence is enriched with the social aspect of language, compared to the Chomskyan view of competence, its main limitation comes from looking at one language at a time rather than multiple languages. In the case of multilingual speakers, it is fundamental to look at the sum of their multiple language capacity in a holistic perspective. Nonetheless, according to some scholars (e.g. Hall, 2019) the term *competence* is not preferred due to the idea of 'homogeneity, permanence, and universality' that it carries (Hall, 2019: 86). He suggests using the term *repertoire* to refer to 'the totality of an individual's language knowledge defining it as conventionalised constellations of semiotic resources for taking action' (Hall, 2019: 86). Interestingly, Cenoz and Gorter (2019) add the pre-modifier expression 'multilingual and multimodal' to the term repertoire to highlight not only the heterogeneous background of multilingual learners and speakers but also the non-linguistic semiotic resources.

For the purpose of the current discussion, it is worth mentioning the difference between the concept of dominant language constellation (DLC) and linguistic repertoire (Lo Bianco & Aronin, 2020). DLC is described as a set of languages that together carry out all the functions of the human language, thus enabling individuals and groups to persist in a multilingual environment. The peculiar aspect of DLC is that it is conceived as a set of languages including only the most expedient languages. On the other hand, the concept of linguistic repertoire refers to all the languages known to an individual or used in a community. DLC and linguistic repertoire are complementary concepts. DLC constitutes an active, working part of a language repertoire and typically comprises three languages. A language repertoire, a kind of linguistic resource or storage, may include a much longer list of languages and skills. DLC applies to both societal language contact and multilingualism and individual multilingual practices.

Recent research on TLA has shown that languages interact among each other, they are multidirectional and that multilingual learners make use of similar strategies when producing written texts in multiple languages (Cenoz & Gorter, 2011). Yet, this suggests the existence of soft boundaries between languages, implying from a pedagogical and theoretical point of view, to switch to the focus from a monolingual to a multilingual perspective. In this way, when conducting research on TLA, the commonalities shared by different languages can be stressed to enhance learners' multilingual repertoire. Additionally, it can be argued that the expression multilingual repertoire, preferred to that of multilingual competence, focuses on aspects that learners already possess rather than something that still needs to be achieved. It highlights learners' knowledge in multiple languages and semiotic systems and its dynamic nature. Nonetheless, this does not imply that the idealised monolingual speaker needs to be replaced with an idealised multilingual learner of additional languages. Indeed, emerging multilinguals come to the process of TLA with a much more complex and diverse repertoire as well as very diverse goals to achieve. As the Douglas Fir Group (2016: 29) maintains, 'language learning is characterised by variability and change. It is a ceaseless moving target'.

The concept of translanguaging is the result of seeing the modern world as a superdiverse environment, also considering online communication, where people make use of all the linguistic and semiotic resources available in the different contexts to achieve the main common goal of communicative functionality. To do so, they resort to different resources, strategies and techniques and, most importantly, they blend and merge all these resources into a broader and unique linguistic system. Accordingly, expressions such as code-switching no longer seem appropriate to describe the linguistic and semiotic reality and practices of multilinguals. Specifically, '(the expression) exhausts the limits of their descriptive and explanatory adequacy in the face of such high complex blends' (Blommaert, 2016: 247). Additionally, the translanguaging approach questions concepts of crosslinguistic influence (CLI) and transfer because such notions assume the existence of different subsystems that have been overcome by this view. In other words, the notion of code-switching is abandoned by supporters of translanguaging since, by definition, there are no codes left in this theory.

Sayer (2013) explains the importance of shifting from code-switching to translanguaging in pedagogical, social and political terms. Yet, what seems to portray an ideal learning environment is rejected. More specifically, in his words:

> Translanguaging can help students figure out a particular vocabulary item or scientific concept, but it also allows students to participate in identity performances with their classmates that socialise them into the classroom, co-constructing them as component members of the group. (Sayer, 2013: 70)

On the other hand, Canagarajah (2013) resorts to the expression *code-meshing* or translanguaging to substitute for code-switching as both writers and readers negotiate the meaning of texts. In particular, the author maintains that students incorporate words and expressions from the different languages they know. Also, he refers to examples of code-meshing from academic writing to show that it is an accepted practice even outside the classroom.

The main reason why multilingualism has been seen to have a social dimension is that multilinguals learn languages by engaging in language practices in a social context. Hence, the role of the social context is central to the discussion of language boundaries. It should be noted that the expression translanguaging was first used to refer to a pedagogical practice in Wales where the languages being studied were English and Welsh (Williams, 1994, 1996, 2000). The main aim was to revitalise the Welsh language in the context of Welsh–English bilingual programmes, drawing attention to the systematic input and output in the two languages. These latter are very different from a typological point of view: English is a Germanic language and Welsh is a Celtic language. The quantitative input of Welsh and English varies depending on the relative use of each language as the language of instruction. A similar situation can be found in the Basque country in Spain, with Spanish and Basque. Even though Welsh and Basque are recognised as languages of instruction from primary school, they still represent minority languages within their social contexts of use. Accordingly, all speakers become fluent in the majority languages, i.e. English and Spanish, whereas the minority languages are mastered and used to different extents.

As already mentioned, in recent years, different scholars have questioned the concept of languages as separate identities. Nonetheless, as Ortega (2019: 31) points out, 'languages are often identified and treated by speakers as labelled and separate at the conscious level'. Even though there are considerable differences between the languages involved in the example provided, i.e. Basque and Spanish, the two languages have influenced each other because they have been in contact for centuries. The direction of the influence is from the majority to the minority language, mastered by all speakers, and involves all linguistic levels from phonology to syntax. Hence, because of this influence, the boundaries between languages in one's multilingual repertoire have been conceived as weaker and softer.

4.3 Translanguaging and Minority Languages

Advocates of the translanguaging approach, as already argued, question the notions of code-switching and CLI and the existence of boundaries between languages and, most importantly, call for radical changes in pedagogical practices. Specifically, they maintain that a translanguaging approach is needed in heterogeneous and superdiverse contexts based on the assumption that monolingualism in education is an ideology that is related to nationalism and racism (Berthele, 2020: 17). Following this line, translanguaging seems to be particularly advisable for those instructional contexts involving minority languages. Indeed, the fluid use of languages which breaks the strict separation of ideologies, typical of monolingual education, both outside and inside school contexts, is crucial for communities with a considerable presence of minority languages. Otheguy *et al.* (2015: 283), for instance, argue that the reason why translanguaging can be beneficial for those communities is that 'it helps to disrupt the socially constructed language hierarchies that are responsible for the suppression of the languages of many minoritised peoples'.

Nonetheless, for these contexts, it is important to consider the asymmetrical relations of power and inequalities since there is a risk of empowering the speakers of the majority languages rather than the other way round. Hence, as Cenoz and Gorter (2017) maintain, some spaces need to be allocated to the minority languages. For this purpose, they advance five principles to develop translanguaging practices in school contexts dealing with one or multiple minority languages:

(1) Design functional breathing spaces for using the minority language.
(2) Develop the need to use minority languages through translanguaging.
(3) Use emergent multilinguals' resources to reinforce all languages by developing MLA.
(4) Enhance language awareness.
(5) Link spontaneous translanguaging to pedagogical activities.

As Cenoz and Gorter (2019) note, there is a significant difference in the way minority languages can be preserved nowadays. If, in the past, language isolation and monolingual ideologies may have been useful for the preservation and revival of minority languages, today they no longer benefit minority language speakers in the same way. Instead, they can even be seen as counterproductive. The translanguaging approach must be adopted with careful consideration of the characteristic of the sociolinguistic contexts in which it is applied. Otherwise, the authors maintain, it can even result in language loss. Thus, especially where language minorities are involved, adopting translanguaging practices means recognising, first of all, the diverse language and meaning-making practices as well as the local histories of those communities who language and translanguage differently from the monoglossic systems.

4.3.1 Defining minority and heritage language learners

If, on the one hand, earlier pedagogical programmes had made reference to language education for 'bilinguals' or 'native speakers', the establishment of HL and minority language education as a field, on the other, has brought to the fore a new label and category that needs to be clarified: 'heritage language learner'. Indeed, there is no universal understanding of just what the terms 'heritage language' and 'heritage language learner' mean. Definitions differ on whether the primary focus is on the languages, their societal status or individuals' linguistic proficiency. Researchers adopting the original Canadian usage by defining HLs as 'languages other than the national language(s)' (Duff & Li, 2009: 4) are generally more attuned to the sociopolitical status of a given language or to the collective rights and needs of the speakers of that language as a group.

It is in this research and policy context that there are also ongoing debates about whether terms such as 'ancestral language', 'minority language' or 'community language' are equivalent or preferable to 'heritage language'. In the current work, no conceptual distinction has been adopted between heritage, home and minority language. On the other hand, researchers focusing more specifically on educational policy and curricular design tend to give greater weight to linguistic proficiency and cultural connections in their discussions of who should be classified as a HL speaker: either all individuals with an ancestral or family tie to the language – even if they have extremely limited or no proficiency in the language – or just those who have some productive and/or receptive ability. Implicit in the construct of the HL speaker is the notion that the individual's HL proficiency has been developed prior to their exposure to the national language, although this is not always technically the case. It can be noted that while the emphasis is on the individual speaker, language status generally is also implicated in proficiency-based definitions.

Generally speaking, HL learners have been defined as individuals who 'have familial or ancestral ties to a particular language and who exert their agency in determining whether or not they are heritage language learners of that heritage language and heritage culture' (Hornberger & Wang, 2008: 27). This definition reminds us of the centrality of affective issues, particularly those surrounding identity, belonging and connections to the HL and culture. Indeed, according to Agnes He (2006: 7), identity is 'the centerpiece rather than the background of heritage language development'. Definitions of HL learners such as Hornberger and Wang's (2008), more focused on affiliation and identity, are considered broad definitions in contrast with the so-called narrow definitions of HLs, which hinge on linguistic knowledge. Speaking to the latter type of definition, Guadalupe Valdés observes:

> Foreign language educators use the term to refer to a language student who is raised in a home where a non-English language is spoken, who speaks or at least understands the language, and who is to some degree bilingual in that language and in English. (Valdés, 2001: 38)

4.3.2 Minority language learners as peculiar bilinguals and multilinguals

In recent years, the term heritage language has been broadly used to refer to non-societal and non-majority languages spoken by groups often known as linguistic minorities. Those members of linguistic minorities who are concerned about the study, maintenance and revitalisation of their minority languages have been referred to as HL students. Such minorities include populations who are either indigenous to a particular region of a present-day nation-state (e.g. Aborigines in Australia, speakers of Breton in France, Kurds in Turkey, Iran and Iraq) or populations who have migrated to areas other than their own regions or nations of origin (e.g. Mexicans in the United States, Turks in Germany, Moroccans in Spain, Pakistanis in England).

The label minority languages or HLs includes a broad variety of languages with different features. On the one hand, indigenous languages that are often endangered and in danger of disappearing (e.g. Scots Gaelic, Maori and Romani), and on the other, world languages commonly spoken in many other regions of the world (e.g. Spanish in the United States, Arabic in France). In terms of context of acquisition, speakers who may acquire and use two or more languages in order to meet their everyday communicative needs in such settings have been referred to as circumstantial bilinguals/multilinguals (Valdés & Figueroa, 1994). In contrast, elite or elective bilinguals/multilinguals learn a second language (L2) in classroom settings and have few opportunities to use the language for genuine communication.

Circumstantial bilingualism/multilingualism is typical of populations who generally occupy subaltern positions in particular settings, whether they are indigenous minorities in established nation-states (e.g. Bretons, Samis and Kurds) or other border crossers such as migrants, refugees, nomads and exiles. The following observation by Fishman is very meaningful to understand the social implications as well as the perception that lay speakers have of language prestige:

> Many Americans have long been of the opinion that bilingualism is a good thing if it was acquired via travel (preferably to Paris) or via formal education (preferably at Harvard) but it is a bad thing if it was acquired from one's immigrant parents or grandparents. (Fishman, 1966: 122–123)

4.4 The Monolingual Bias in Language Education Research

As Grosjean (1985) and Cook (1997) have argued, first language (L1)/L2 users are not two monolinguals in one, but rather specific speakers/hearers who have acquired their two languages in particular contexts and for particular reasons. Viewed from a bilingualist rather than a monolingualist perspective, L1/L2 users have acquired two knowledge systems that they use in order to carry out their particular communicative needs, which may be quite unlike those of monolingual native speakers who use a single language in all communicative interactions. Also, arguing for a bilingualist perspective on L1/L2 users, Grosjean (1997) contended that, at any given moment, bilinguals are in states of activation of their languages and language processing mechanisms that are either monolingual or bilingual. The education system has no special resources for minority language learners. Yet, their point of departure as language learners differs markedly from that of second/foreign language learners (FLL) in many respects. Typically, HL learners find it surprisingly difficult to react in a teaching situation (which may emulate a context they are not accustomed to), they cannot interpret the teacher's didactic intentions and respond accordingly. This is obviously symptomatic of the general problem of HL learners involving insufficient MLA or the missing ability to consciously analyse their home language.

4.5 Heritage Language Education: A Focus on Identity

In contrast with earlier essentialist views that conceived identity as a static characteristic that people have, suggesting that identity is stable and resists change (Ford & Ford, 1994; Giddens, 1991), contemporary social constructivist accounts emphasise that people's sense of themselves and of their relationship to the world is shifting and multiple (Achugar, 2006; Berard, 2005; Norton, 2000). In other words, identities are not fixed within the individual but, instead, are shaped and constrained by macro- and micro-level sociohistorical contexts, including societal ideologies, power relations and institutional policies. Interestingly, Otsuji and Pennycook (2009) try to go beyond the fixed/dynamic dichotomy focusing on the paradoxical practice and space wherein fixity and fluidity coexist with and co-constitute each other. In other words, they argue that it is through the interaction of fixity and fluidity that diverse and dynamic languages, cultures and identities are produced. Fixity and fluidity are considered two concepts in a state of 'symbiotically (re)constituting each other' (Otsuji & Pennycook, 2009: 244).

Hence, language learning is a particularly suitable area in which to investigate the status of identity because languages are instantiated in discourse, and learning a new language involves taking on new ways of being (Canagarajah, 2004; Kanno & Norton, 2003; Norton, 2000, 2005). However, until recently, the study of language learning and identity only focused on L2 learning. It is only in the past decade that scholars have begun to expand this line of inquiry to HL education with multilinguals.

Labels have an impact on how referents are understood and experienced, and they are one way in which identities are discursively produced (Eckert & McConnell-Ginet, 1995). Because the choice of terms has implications for how HL speakers are perceived by others as well as for how they perceive themselves, the association of the term heritage with the past has led some researchers to raise concerns that it positions non-English languages as historical relics. For instance, García's (2005: 605) critique of the shift in US educational policy from bilingual education to HL programmes stresses the backward-looking connotations of the terminological shift, maintaining that 'our multiple identities have been silenced, with one identity reduced to heritage'.

Much HL education in the United States is at least implicitly linked to ethnocultural identity and/or questions of educational equity. Building on this history while also drawing from critical pedagogy, some HL educators have sought to challenge the privileging of an imagined monolingual standard variety and the stigmatisation of heritage speakers for their non-standard or deficient varieties and practices by engaging students in analyses of the relationship of language to identity in discussions of language variation and multilingual practices (Leeman, 2014).

The expansion of research on identity in language educational contexts to include HL education reflects a recognition of the heterogeneity of learners' linguistic backgrounds and identities, as well as the type of investment that learners bring to language study (Norton, 2012). On the other hand, studies of HL education and learners have incorporated some of the theoretical perspectives and contributions from outside the field of HL pedagogy. Social constructivist approaches to identity, for instance, usually include qualitative and ethnographic research methods, allowing a broader understanding of heritage learners' identities (He, 2010) Consequently, it has been acknowledged that HL learners seek to (re)claim an ethnonational identity embodied in the HL, while also revealing that this ideology remains strong among students and teachers in many HL educational contexts (Leeman, 2015). Another valuable outcome of recent research is a rejection of the binary opposition between native speaker and non-native speaker (Valdés, 2005). Nonetheless, it is important to endorse that a HL speaker is also a constructed identity, one that is alternately contrasted to native speakers and non-native speakers, and which can run the risk of being seen as a bounded category, mutually exclusive with, as well as inherently subordinated to, the primary categories of native and non-native.

4.6 Translanguaging and Bilingual Education

Adding to the well-known distinction between subtractive and additive bilingualism, propounded by Lambert (1974), García (2009a) suggests considering another two types of bilingualism that are more realistic and inclusive of the diverse language practices typical of our societies: recursive and dynamic bilingualism. The first highlights the complex and dynamic aspects of the type of bilingualism that characterises ethnolinguistic groups who have experienced substantial language shifts. For these groups that may have experienced language loss at different levels, the author suggests immersion revitalisation bilingual education programmes aimed at integrating their different language practices into a bilingual future. Additionally, another type of programme which particularly suits recursive bilinguals is developmental bilingual education since the ethnolinguistic group is not only multilingual but also conveys different identities.

Dynamic bilingualism, on the other hand, refers to the multiple language interactions and various linguistic interrelationships that occur in multilingual speakers and learners on different scales. In particular, nowadays, many bilingual education programmes include children with diverse language practices who may belong to dominant and non-dominant groups. In this case, García suggests multilingual education programmes based on the use of three or more languages as the media of instruction and in literacy instruction. Again, the most important aspect is considering the linguistic and sociocultural heterogeneity of the speakers.

A translanguaging approach to bilingual education takes into account all the aforementioned contexts, linguistic varieties and, most importantly, learners' different communicative needs and goals when they learn additional languages. As Williams (2002) points out, translanguaging means using one language to reinforce another in order to increase learners' understanding and activities in multiple languages. More specifically, translanguaging, as conceived and used by Williams, refers to a 'pedagogical theory which involves students' learning two languages through a process of deep cognitive bilingual engagement' (García & Li, 2015: 224).

Translanguaging permits the real integration of emergent bilinguals with those bilinguals who display a fuller use of the languages in a classroom setting. The way García (2009) makes use of the term stresses the importance of going beyond the concept of different languages in education. She states 'translanguaging, or engaging in bilingual or multilingual discourse practices, is an approach to bilingualism that is centred not on languages as has been often the case, but on the practices of bilinguals that are readily observable' (García, 2009: 44).

On the inclusive aspect of translanguaging, where multiple linguistic systems and learners are blended together, it is worth recalling García and Kano's (2014) point of view. They consider translanguaging as a process, engaging students and teachers in a complex discursive practice where all languages and students are involved to achieve different educational goals: (1) to develop new language practices that are also able to sustain the old ones; (2) to communicate and convey knowledge in multiple languages; and (3) to break linguistic inequalities by giving voice and space to new sociopolitical realities.

The notion of translanguaging in education focuses on two crucial aspects explored and described by Li Wei (2011): creativity and criticality. 'Creativity is the ability to choose between following and flouting the rules and norms of behaviour, including the use of language' (Li, 2011: 1223). In other words, creativity is seen as breaking the boundaries between old and new, tradition and innovation, what needs to be accepted and what should be changed in language education. Criticality, on the other hand, refers to 'the ability to use available evidence appropriately, systematically and insightfully, to inform considered views of cultural, social, and linguistic phenomena, to question and problematize received wisdom, and to express views adequately through reasoned responses to situations' (García & Li, 2015: 226). These two concepts are interrelated and depend upon each other since one needs to be critical to break existing conventional boundaries. Yet, creativity is necessary for critical thinking to occur.

As a socioeducational process, translanguaging enables students to construct and constantly modify their values as well as their identities both critically and creatively. It allows questioning the traditional conventions in educational processes based on one language only or one language at a time, typical of monolingual or traditional bilingual settings. Indeed, due to the more responsible and sensitive practices of national education systems for the education of children belonging to both dominant majority and minority languages, translanguaging has been increasingly used to overcome the traditional monolingual education system. It is a tool to merge the nation-state educational programmes with the various linguistic and sociocultural histories and realities of students with different languages. For bilingual education programmes, adopting a translanguaging lens means showing a flexible approach between different language policies to engage and enhance students' multilingual and multimodal linguistic repertoire.

A recent study by Aldekoa *et al.* (2020) shows how trilingual teaching interventions, based on the principles of the integrated teaching of languages and translanguaging, are used to effectively promote multilingual skills in the Basque educational context. It was reported to foster the development of oral presentation skills not only in Basque, but also in L1 Spanish and L3 English. The teaching practice involved alternating between the three languages with a preference for Basque, the minority language in this case. Oral presentations were produced by the 16-year-old trilingual students before and after the teaching intervention. The authors concluded that carefully planned language alternation and the integration of languages are an effective tool to promote multilingual development including the minority language.

To achieve this goal, it is fundamental to put the minority language alongside the majority language reserving a space where minority and majority languages are not in competition. Within this translanguaging space, as Li (2011) points out, it is also necessary to prompt students to act creatively and critically. In particular, educational practices must aim at the cognitive involvement of children and at the development of more sophisticated MLA. 'In these translanguaging spaces linguistically diverse students are able to co-construct their language expertise, recognise each other as resources, and act on their knowing, doing, and languaging' (García & Li, 2015: 228).

More specifically, the translanguaging space, as theorised by Li (2011), is created by and for translingual practices to break down, through interaction, the conventional dichotomies between macro and micro, societal and individual. It enables multilingual learners and users to integrate all those linguistic codes, separated through different social and political practices. Translanguaging enables the creation of a social space which brings together different aspects of one's personal history, identity experience, etc. Nonetheless, it can be argued that these educational spaces rarely exist in established school systems. As a linguistic theory, translanguaging perfectly portrays the actual situation of how real individuals convey meanings in their everyday lives, in different communicative contexts. Schools, as a pedagogical practice, are seldom used to mediate complex cognitive activities.

Translanguaging is a practice that transforms the whole education system from both teachers' and students' perspectives. From the students' perspective, translanguaging has been seen as a practice used to learn even though it is not officially recognised as an educational pedagogy. For learners, developing new language skills is a challenging cognitive activity since, as discussed in previous sections, it requires rebuilding the whole linguistic and semiotic repertoire. It involves a coexistence between old and new language practices that are not simply added to the system. It affects and transforms the way learners act, communicate and make and convey new meanings. Hence, it is not a mere quantitative difference but involves a significant qualitative change which reshapes the whole cognitive and linguistic profile of additional language learners.

Translanguaging highlights the interconnection between traditionally understood language systems and other, more inclusive, human communication systems. As human beings' knowledge of languages cannot be parted from their knowledge of human relations and human social interactions, Pinker (1994) conveys the metaphor of language instinct to refer to human beings' innate capacity of acquiring languages. This idea has been taken and expanded by Li Wei (2016) with the notion of translanguaging instinct to stress the importance of mediated interaction in everyday life. In other words, the multisensory and multimodal process of language learning and language use. A translanguaging instinct drives humans to go beyond narrowly defined languages and cultures to achieve effective communication.

Translanguaging also has important consequences for multilingual education policies and practices. If, on the one hand, the natural drive to learn languages is innate, on the other, the modal resources for language learning vary through the course of life and are not equally available all the time. In L1 acquisition, infants infer meanings by combining the sounds, images and actions around them. In bilingual L1 acquisition, where CLI is involved, the effort is to associate the target word with a specific context or addressee where either language is acceptable. The more the communicative task becomes complex, the more people show a natural tendency to combine and resort to multiple resources available. They also learn how to adapt different types of resources and learning strategies to different communicative needs. This has been seen to result in a functional differentiation of different linguistic resources for different purposes as well as between cognitive, semiotic and linguistic skills.

A number of translanguaging teaching practices are explicitly presented in the CUNY-NYSIEB guide (City University of New York-New York State's Initiative for Emergent Bilinguals; Celic & Seltzer, 2011). The first step is empowering students to use their languages via small actions and adaptations, such as making those languages visible in the classroom or by learning to say 'hello' in different languages (García & Li, 2014). Students are encouraged to complete writing assignments using all of their linguistic resources (Kiramba, 2017). Moreover, they can work in pairs using the language(s) of their choosing. This is particularly fruitful between students who have different levels of the language of schooling, as based on the principles of scaffolding (García & Li, 2014). However, in contexts where this practice is difficult to implement, i.e. where languages are not equally represented in the classroom, students can be encouraged to compare languages, such as by searching for cognates in different languages for vocabulary development and morphological awareness (Ticheloven *et al.*, 2019).

Thus, this total rebuilding and retransforming the way of learning new structures, contents and strategies enable us to go from the concept of linguistic transfer in bilingual education, introduced by Cummins (1978), to the concept of integration of language practices on behalf of learners. Most importantly, the new language practices constituting their own unique repertoire do not belong to the school or home settings. Rather, they belong to the learners and to their peculiar way of acting, learning and languaging. For emergent bilingual students, that is for those who are still in the process of developing new language practices, translanguaging means accessing new knowledge through language practices that they have already mastered. In other words, they deal with new texts by applying old and familiar languages. At the same time, the more they get into the new language system(s), the more they can show what they already know by merging and blending tradition and innovation creatively and critically.

One of the most interesting aspects of translanguaging, from the students' perspective, is the flexibility of selecting the language practice they need depending on the communicative context in which they use the language. It may be the case that bilingual learners, when talking or conveying information found in a written text, make use of meaning-making resources that are not officially found in the classroom setting and might not be understood by teachers. This leads to another crucial feature of bilingual learners conveyed by translanguaging, i.e. the self-efficacy they show when dealing with strategies that enable them to regulate their own learning at their own pace.

Indeed, since knowledge is acquired interpersonally, it needs to be mediated by peers and teachers in order to be internalised. Accordingly, translanguaging has been seen to enhance metatalk, metacognition and whispered private speech. There is a variety of ways that bilingual students make use of translanguaging practices and techniques to learn, at different points on the bilingual continuum. As reported in a study by García and Kano (2014), emergent bilinguals tended to use translanguaging as they were dependent on their expertise with other language practices in order to complete the task. More experienced bilinguals, on the other hand, demonstrated greater autonomy and ability to self-regulate. However, in both cases, the two languages were continuously activated during the task, at different levels. In addition, all the participants demonstrated autonomy and control of the language, linguistic awareness of their linguistic needs and were conscious of their strengths and limitations.

In another influential work on a two-way dual language bilingual kindergarten, García (2011) considers how five-year-old children translanguage when entering school speaking only English or only Spanish. In the process of developing their English–Spanish bilingualism, the young learners have been reported to use six metafunctions:

(1) to mediate understanding among each other;
(2) to co-construct meaning of what the other is saying;
(3) to construct meaning within oneself;
(4) to include others;
(5) to exclude others;
(6) to demonstrate knowledge.

As discussed in the previous chapters, one of the most influential aspects of schooling is the development of literacy which also enhances the MLA of language by turning language into a visual object to manipulate and consciously analyse. Particularly, through translanguaging practices, this skill assumes an even greater importance due to the development and use of learners' entire semiotic and linguistic repertoire.

4.6.1 Translanguaging applied to heritage language education

Translanguaging has proven to be an effective pedagogical practice in a variety of educational contexts where the school language or the language of instruction is different from the learners' L1 (Li, 2018). Over the last years, it has been advocated as a language theory and a pedagogical practice that empowers both learners and teachers, transforms power relations and focuses the process of teaching and learning on making meaning, enhancing experience and developing identities. More specifically, it deliberately breaks the artificial and ideological divides between indigenous versus immigrant, majority versus minority and target versus mother tongue languages (García, 2009). In their work, Creese and Blackledge (2015) focus on recent educational practices, based on translanguaging, examining the role of identity. They see identities as socially constructed in interaction and consider the relationship between language and identities in complex and superdiverse contexts of communication. In particular, they report examples of translanguaging practice taken from empirical research on a Panjabi complementary community language (or HL) school in Birmingham, UK. The authors highlight the role of teachers as mediators propounding the use of both English and Panjabi as acceptable classroom practices. A teacher asks students to write sentences about what they did on holidays. Students write a sentence in Panjabi and the teacher uses both resources to introduce the past tense, encouraging students to freely express themselves in both languages. Importantly, the teacher provides examples of grammatically correct sentences in both languages to reinforce the students' MLA comparing English and Panjabi structures.

A translanguaging approach applied to research on multilingualism and HL, as discussed, challenges the monolingual bias conceiving languages purely in terms of level of attainment. Instead, it is advisable to switch the focus from the target language(s) to the multilingual learner as:

> someone who is aware of the existence of the political entities of named languages, has acquired some of their structural features, and has a Translanguaging instinct that enables a resolution of the differences, discrepancies, inconsistencies, and ambiguities and manipulates them for strategic gains. (Li, 2018: 19)

More explicitly, in classroom settings, as García (2011) notes, translanguaging goes beyond code-switching and translation because it refers to the process in which students perform bilingually in the myriad multimodal ways of classrooms – reading, writing, taking notes, discussing, signing and so on. For example, multilingual learners in a translanguaging class may take notes in their L1, summarise in their L2 and paraphrase in their third or additional language.

4.7 Unitary vs Crosslinguistic Translanguaging Orientations: A Theoretical Debate

An important theoretical debate on translanguaging deals with the evolution of the theory over the past decade into a strong or unitary version which carried, in Cummin's (2021: 271) own words, 'a considerable amount of extraneous conceptual baggage that risks undermining its overall credibility'. In particular, according to Cummins, the main concepts conveyed by the advocates of the Unitary Translanguage Theory represent a distorted evolution of the original framework and can be summarised as follows:

- Languages are 'invented' and do not exist as discrete 'countable' entities (e.g. Makoni & Pennycook, 2007).
- The multilingual's linguistic system is internally undifferentiated and unitary, reflecting the fact that languages have no linguistic and cognitive reality (e.g. García, 2009).
- Code-switching is an illegitimate monoglossic construct because it assumes the existence of two separate linguistic systems (e.g. Otheguy et al., 2015, 2019).
- Additive bilingualism is an illegitimate monoglossic construct, assuming the existence of two separate languages that are added together in bilingual individuals (e.g. García, 2009).

Cummins (2021) considers the aforementioned points problematic, unsupported by empirical research, logically inconsistent and, most importantly, undermining the potential contribution of translanguaging to an effective and equitable pedagogy. Indeed, he maintains that the evolution of translanguaging theories, particularly referring to the works of García and colleagues discussed in this chapter (e.g. García, 2009; García & Li, 2014), is characterised by an inherent contradiction. That is, they claim that the development of their theories is influenced by two main sources: the aforementioned work by Williams (2002) in Wales, who coined the term, and the work by Makoni and Pennycook (2005) assuming that languages are invented and cannot be considered as separate identities. The contradiction noticed by Cummins deals with the acknowledgement, on behalf of García and colleagues, of the existence of languages as social entities but not within our linguistic and cognitive system.

In regard to the monoglossic construct of additive bilingualism, Makoni and Pennycook (2005: 148) maintain that 'there is a disconcerting similarity between monolingualism and additive bilingualism in so far as both are founded on notions of language as objects [...] additive bilingualism and multilingualism are at best pluralisation of monolingualism'. That is to say, they argue that the educational promotion of multilingualism and additive bilingualism is based on the monolingual assumptions about language that these same constructs aim to question. Cummins advocates an interesting disambiguation of these claims resorting to the dichotomies between heteroglossic (dynamic) and monoglossic (static) orientations towards bilingualism.

The most controversial issue arising from the Unitary Translanguage Theory is that the adoption of Makoni and Pennycook's point of view logically entails the rejection of the original Welsh concept of translanguaging. That is, it rejects the construction of additive bilingualism and teaching for productive contact between languages. According to the Welsh theorists, Welsh and English are two distinct languages from a cognitive and linguistic point of view. On the other hand, advocates of the Unitary Translanguage Theory consider the original Welsh concept as belonging to the category of weak or crosslinguistic translanguaging theory and as monoglossic (or static) in orientation. Nonetheless, the Welsh researchers still acknowledge the importance of crosslinguistic transfer for additive bilingualism and teaching. Instead, they acknowledge the cognitive and linguistic reality of languages and the advantages of additive bilingualism. See, for example, the point of view conveyed by Lewis *et al.*:

> Pedagogical translanguaging allows more effective learning due to cross-language semantic remapping that occurs when the encoded information in one language is retrieved to enable production in the other language. (Lewis *et al.*, 2012a: 650)

Hence, despite the general consensus on the legitimacy and the potential benefits of translanguaging as an effective pedagogical theory and practice, a number of theorists have considered the aforementioned claims by García and colleagues as inherently contradictory. Adopting, at the same time, the positions of the Welsh theorists on the one hand, and Makoni and Pennycook's view, they endorse the notion of additive bilingualism, code-switching and crosslinguistic transfer as belonging to a monoglossic and static paradigm. Consequently, this view considers additive bilingualism as an obstacle to the development of minority students' academic growth: 'Standard languages and additive bilingualism have been used as instruments to minoritise the language practices of some bilinguals and rendering them as deficient' (García, 2020: 16).

On the other hand, Cummins (2021) convincingly disputes such notions, maintaining that crosslinguistic interdependence and teaching for transfer does not reflect monoglossic ideologies. Accordingly, additive bilingualism does not convey notions of appropriateness and raciolinguistic ideologies. In particular, the author claims that the theoretical framework advanced by advocates of the crosslinguistic theoretical orientation acknowledges the importance of additive bilingualism for teaching in instructional settings involving minority languages. More specifically, he refers to three main teaching goals:

a. to enhance and value minority students' bilingualism and biliteracy;
b. to actively build students' awareness about languages in academic contexts;
c. to teach for the transfer of concepts, skills and learning strategies across languages.

Thus, despite the opposing views distinguishing translanguaging theorists on the legitimacy of notions referring to code-switching and the separation of languages, what is widely acknowledged is the validity of interpersonal and pedagogical translanguaging, i.e. the fluid communicative use of the individual's entire linguistic repertoire. However, long before the spread of translanguaging theories, there were numerous examples, reported by Cummins (2021), of educators exploiting the multilingual resources of minority language students. Over the last 30 years, teachers and educators have documented their experiences and instructional initiatives (see Chapter 5) collaborating with university researchers. This fruitful collaboration between teaching and the research field has demonstrated the effectiveness of what will be called pedagogical translanguaging to:

> scaffold higher levels of academic performance, build critical language awareness, engage students' actively with literacy in both their home and school languages, and affirm students' identities. (Cummins, 2021: 273)

Hence, the theoretical and original framework of translanguaging, as both a theory and practice of language, aimed at mobilising students' multilingual and multimodal repertoire is supported by several studies highlighting the benefits of connecting students' personal experiences, involving their home languages in their school's practices to reinforce their levels of bilingualism and biliteracy, recognising and valuing their multicultural identities and enhancing their multilingual oral and written skills. In other words, 'the construct of translanguaging (broadly defined) can be viewed as legitimate from the perspectives of empirical adequacy, logical coherence, and consequential validity' (Cummins, 2021: 273).

4.8 Conclusion

To conclude, translanguaging offers a 'practical theory of language', to use Li Wei's (2018) words, considering the complexity and multifaced linguistic reality of our time. It enables the exploitation of multilingual and multimodal resources available to multilingual speakers and learners. Furthermore, as discussed, in its broader meaning which includes the principles of additive bilingualism, it is a fundamental tool to overcome the traditional dichotomies from the past, typical of monolingual education systems. Indeed, since the separation between languages and other cognitive domains is far from being a psychological reality, the one-to-one relationship between languages and identities needs to be reconsidered too. Indeed, a common feature distinguishing human ways of communicating and interacting is the alternation of different codes, oral and written, and different linguistic varieties, across different dimensions and styles, to move dynamically among different languages. That is, language users, in their everyday social interaction, are constantly called on to resort to different varieties, styles, registers and semiotic systems to achieve specific communicative goals.

Most importantly, this mixture of tones, styles, registers and semiotic resources builds a new identity which cannot be associated with the identity of speakers of particular languages. From a translanguaging perspective, understanding which language is being spoken becomes irrelevant. Instead, translanguaging challenges the conventional approaches to multilingualism and multilingual education since its main interest is a better understanding of how multiple language speakers make use of their multilingual and multisemiotic repertoire to communicate and socially interact in their daily lives. This perspective allows a thorough exploration of the human mind and how it resorts to creative and dynamic practices while engaging with multilingual and multimodal resources.

Beyond the inclusion of different language practices, translanguaging can also be considered an effective tool against ostracism and racism towards minority language groups. By merging different representations, histories and backgrounds, it has the potential to break the native speaker ideal of a standard language to achieve via schooling. Indeed, translanguaging practices support and include those speakers of minority languages often stigmatised and excluded from educational programmes. It has the potential to develop more sophisticated discourse and a deeper comprehension of multilingual texts, to produce complex texts, to evaluate and enhance prior linguistic and cultural knowledge and, most importantly, to include all learners' voices, as recognised by teachers and educators first. Interestingly, Gutièrrez (2008) describes instructors' use of hybrid language practices in a summer programme for young migrants to incite and support students' own repertoires of language practices. In other words, what the author defines as the 'sociocritical literacy' required of teachers who adopt translanguaging as a pedagogical practice.

Thus, the crucial concern is to look at how students in multilingual classrooms deploy various aspects of their translingual repertoires to construct and index multifaceted identities, including locally meaningful identities, HL education and identities that are not defined with reference to the HL, as well as how these various indices and identities intersect. Hence, the broader and fluid linguistic repertoire and the type of resources needed, available and exploited during the whole acquisition process need to be analysed and included. The learning strategies combined and used by multilingual learners for specific linguistic tasks need to be considered to thoroughly understand the peculiar nature of third or additional language acquisition and learning.

Nonetheless, it can be argued that on the one hand, as a linguistic theory, translanguaging perfectly portrays the actual situation of how real individuals convey meanings in their everyday lives, in different communicative contexts. On the other, as a pedagogical practice, it is not applied enough in schools to mediate complex cognitive activities requiring multiple linguistic resources. Thus, the challenge is to understand the obstacles encountered by teachers and learners and try to build an innovative, more inclusive, translanguaging space aimed at meeting the realistic communicative needs of multilingual learners in educational settings too. To implement translanguaging as a pedagogical practice, raising awareness among teachers, parents and educators is paramount to convey the benefits of this educational approach. On the other hand, more research is needed to highlight the reasons why it has not been sufficiently extended as an educational practice.

5 From Bilingual to Multilingual Education: Teaching, Assessing and Testing Trends

5.1 Introduction

As discussed in the previous chapters, the acknowledgement of the sociolinguistic reality that the majority of the world's population is to some extent multilingual has led to considerable changes in the language education field. There have been attempts to shift from a monolingual to a multilingual perspective regarding the way multilingual learners are conceived, categorised and assessed in multilingual classrooms. Previous and traditional monolingual and bilingual education programmes were mainly characterised by a focus on code-mixing and crosslinguistic influence, especially in early bilinguals, and on the concept of proficiency distinguishing balanced/unbalanced bilingualism. In the last decades, however, the main issue evaluated by researchers and policymakers has been the concept of multicompetence (Aronin, 2016). It takes into account each individuals' total language repertoire from a holistic and dynamic perspective and it is suitable to portray and analyse the wide variety of sociolinguistic backgrounds typical of multilingual communities, where different first languages (L1s) coexist in the same educational context.

The notion of multicompetence was originally formulated by Cook (1991, 1992, 2015) in reaction to the concept of monocompetence which aimed at evaluating a native-like proficiency in a bilingual or multilingual speaker. The author observed a lack of linguistic labels to refer to the coexistence of the L1 and an interlanguage in the mind. He suggested using the term multicompetence to describe the state of integration of language knowledge in the mind. Indeed, he maintained that 'at one level, multicompetence is undeniable; as L2 users do not have two heads, their minds must be different at some level of abstraction' (Cook, 1991: 112). It is in this first phase that he defined the concept as a 'compound state of a mind with two grammars'. However, in a more recent work, Cook has reformulated the notion of multicompetence, viewing a second language (L2) user/speaker as a whole person with an entire language repertoire.

Accordingly, in his latest definition, he describes the concept as 'the overall system of a mind or a community that uses more than one language' (Cook, 2015: 2).

Thus, research on multilingualism from a holistic perspective considers all individuals' languages as a whole and makes a further distinction between L2 learners and learners of a third language (L3) or more for all the cognitive and linguistic reasons already discussed in the previous chapters. This new conceptualisation of languages and of the language learning process itself resulted in new pedagogical approaches, namely plurilingual (or multilingual) (Council of Europe, 2001). The latter questions the notion of isolated languages, focuses on learners' multilingual repertoires and promotes multilingualism and multiculturalism in the classroom (Beacco *et al.*, 2010). One of the most interesting outcomes of plurilingual approaches is that not only the learners' repertoires but also the teachers' linguistic competences, assessment strategies and resources are rebuilt. Indeed, plurilingual approaches are described as 'making use of the learners' first and other languages to teach more effectively' (Otwinowska-Kasztelanic, 2014: 102). Among the teaching practices, they include the alternation of languages, conscious crosslinguistic comparison and transfer, metalinguistic awareness (MLA) strategies, code-switching and cognates (Kucukali, 2021). In addition, the use of English as a lingua franca between learners' native language and their other languages, exploiting similarities, is suggested to improve and facilitate language learning and teaching (Otwinowska-Kasztelanic, 2014).

5.2 The Monolingual and Bilingual Bias in Multilingual Testing and Assessment

The focus of this chapter is to analyse the challenges of teaching, testing and assessing learners in multilingual educational contexts. Multilingual testing and assessment have improved considerably in the last decades due to the higher level of attention devoted to this field of research. This was due to a number of sociolinguistic and educational factors including the perceived and acknowledged need of policymakers, researchers and educators to integrate immigrant students into mainstream education programmes and to adapt the assessment tools to the diverse varieties of language backgrounds, educational contexts and geographic origins characterising multilingual classrooms. Nonetheless, despite the step forward compared to monolingual assessment practices, as De Angelis (2021) argues, most academic discussions still focus on speakers of two languages, including bilingual assessment and testing needs in homogeneous settings where the amount and quality of input received in each language are equal (i.e. balanced bilingualism). Hence, the majority of testing material developed in the last decades has been tailored to the specific needs of bilingual speakers and learners and does not seem suitable to test and assess multilinguals.

The author maintains that finding the right solution that would be flexible enough to meet the needs of a more heterogeneous population, considering both individual variability and different linguistic contexts, is not an easy task. Indeed, most scholars seem to belong to either the traditional or the holistic approach, that is, two polar extremes incompatible with each other. On the one hand, traditional approaches to testing and assessment are characterised by the use of monolingual tools to assess multilingual speakers ignoring that the language of the test may not be familiar to all test takers. On the other hand, holistic approaches recognise the limits of monolingual testing tools and suggest the use of tests written in multiple languages. However, this cannot be considered a viable or effective solution when more than three languages are involved.

Hence, considering the complexity of multilingual testing and assessment, finding a unique solution to employ in all multilingual contexts, where diverse linguistic profiles are included, does not seem to be feasible. In her recent work, De Angelis (2021) suggests overcoming these dichotomies with a third approach, i.e. an integrated approach to testing and assessment of multilinguals. After analysing the complexity of multilingual populations as well as the limits of the traditional and holistic approaches, she proposes to reject existing barriers, introducing greater flexibilities in the way tests are designed, administered, scored and interpreted. Indeed, tests in multiple languages require much more effort and time on the part of test designers and teachers. In some cases, test content needs to be simplified, including visual forms, or translated into the other languages of the test takers. However, one cannot assume that all teachers have developed the considerable level of linguistic awareness required to make a test simpler or to translate it. If, on the one hand, assessing academic content in multiple languages is an ethically noble and fair principle, on the other, teachers face numerous practical obstacles that make the tests difficult to design, administer and interpret.

Good quality tests must adhere to the principles of validity, inclusivity, viability and accessibility (VIVA) (De Angelis, 2021). Validity refers to the accuracy of predictions from the interpretation of test scores. Thus, a good quality test must demonstrate construct validity showing that the test is able to measure all the stated factors of investigation even though it is a simplified or translated version. That is, they must successfully provide versions of similar difficulties in multiple languages. The criterion of inclusivity refers to the addressees of the test. In the specific case of multilingual tests, linguistically and culturally heterogeneous speakers and learners who may show different levels of proficiency, contexts and methods of instruction in each language. The third criterion mentioned is probably one of the most challenging, i.e. viability, in that it must offer a workable option. The more languages involved in the test design, the lower its viability. Finally, the last criterion characterising multilingual tests is accessibility; it must be easy to understand by all test takers, including those with lower proficiency levels in the language of instruction and students must feel confident to access their knowledge resources to take the test. These resources include personal language or content knowledge as well as the use of linguistic support. Bearing in mind that meeting all the VIVA criteria is a challenging objective for teachers and test takers, they can still work as a guide and a point of reference to design and administer multilingual tests.

The aforementioned integrating approach to multilingual testing and assessment aims to be a flexible solution to record students' proficiency levels and linguistic progress by referring to all the gathered information about the participants. The basic assumption of this approach is that the combination of different types of information allows test designers and teachers to make better decisions when dealing with multilingual tests, from the design to the interpreting phase. The author distinguishes between two crucial aspects, that is designing, administering and scoring multilingual tests on the one hand, and assessing multilingual individuals on the other. Indeed, she observes that several scholars in the field of multiple language acquisition have started to highlight the need to find test design techniques that are suitable for multilinguals and that guidelines on large-scale assessment have recently been published by the International Test Commission (2019). These guidelines describe considerations relevant to the assessment of test takers in or across countries or regions that are linguistically or culturally diverse. They were developed by a committee of experts to help inform test developers, psychometricians, test users and test administrators about fairness issues in support of the fair and valid assessment of linguistically or culturally diverse populations. Nonetheless, if, on the one hand, these guidelines represent an important step forward since they aim to make the tests more accessible and inclusive to meet a variety of linguistic needs, on the other, test scores and interpretation have not been adequately adapted to multilingual test takers' profile. Tests' interpretation is a crucial part of the test that often risks being overlooked. A test provides information on students' progress and performance but, if incorrectly interpreted, it cannot be considered a reliable tool. Indeed, De Angelis (2021) points out that:

> Tests must not only be designed with sufficient sensitivity towards linguistically and culturally diverse students but must also be scored and interpreted using all relevant information about the test takers. Without this last step, unfairness and inequality are likely to occur. (2021: 66)

To respond to the problem of insufficient adaptations of testing and assessing tools that do not take into account test takers' particular profiles and backgrounds, the integrated approach combines information about both the test and the test takers because both types of information are of fundamental importance during the assessment process. Hence, the four key components of the test deal with the way tests are designed, administered, scored and interpreted. They are designed to address the specific needs of linguistically and culturally diverse populations. In addition, tests are administered in multiple modalities based on the different contexts, and are scored by multilingual researchers. Finally, they are interpreted referring to the participants' linguistic background and living environment.

Importantly, each phase is characterised by a high degree of flexibility since test takers can choose to adopt an approach that goes from monolingualism to multilingualism depending on the specific purpose of the test and on the factor under investigation. The most interesting phase that is worth discussing in more detail is the test interpretation. De Angelis' main concern is whether students are being compared according to their language background and, where relevant, the languages spoken within the living community. She insists on the meaninglessness of test scores without a correct and reliable interpretation. In testing, a number of issues have been raised against comparing the monolingual and multilingual performance because of the discussed monolingual bias propounding an idealised native speaker as a point of reference. If, on the one hand, the perfect solution was to provide test takers with multilingual-by-design tests, on the other, it must be acknowledged that it is not always possible due to the mentioned logistic problems when assessing multilinguals. According to De Angelis, a more realistic and easier solution is:

> Stop comparing students who are clearly different in terms of language background and who may live in communities where different language practice expose them to a different quantity and quality of input. (De Angelis, 2021: 81)

She suggests an alternative approach where students are compared on the basis of their language profile and their community context instead of comparing them according to hypothetical group memberships, such as the classroom, since they do not necessarily share the same features. To explain the implications of a failure in classifying multilinguals into dichotomous groups, the author provides an enlightening example of students of Ladin schools in South Tyrol who live in multilingual contexts and are functional multilinguals. In standardised testing, these students cannot be classified as immigrants because they have never moved from their place of residence. Instead, they are considered native speakers when grouped in a test design, even though the language of the test is not their L1. Most importantly, their scores are interpreted in comparison with those of native speakers at the national level or native speakers of surrounding areas. Hence, to avoid any pressure on Ladin students in South Tyrol when asked to perform like native speakers, it would be reasonable to assess their linguistic progress comparing them with other functional multilinguals.

Thus, improving the scoring and interpretation process in multilingual testing seems to be a crucial aspect to enhance research with multilingual populations. Alternative classification methods are needed such as grouping participants according to their language background and the languages spoken in the living community. In her work, De Angelis (2021) examines the attempts made to avoid any comparison between students whose L1 is the language of testing and students with a different L1. A second factor highlighted is the language exposure to different languages within the community. This is particularly relevant in contexts where several languages are spoken on a daily basis, such as multilingual communities with immigrants coming from different areas. Indeed, not only do students speak multiple languages but they are also exposed to a number of other languages in different environments including school, family and the community. From an assessment perspective, it is interesting to focus on the impact of several types and amounts of language exposure on academic performance.

Gathercole *et al.* (2013) conducted a study grouping students according to their language background in Wales, where English and Welsh are both spoken officially within the community. In particular, they classified students according to patterns of language use in the home and school context. The number and type of languages spoken in the home were crucial and linked to students' performance. Also, the study underlined the importance of including exposure to normed tests since it allows us to understand whether children's performance falls within the normal range for their particular cohort. Nonetheless, considering that this study was conducted in a bilingual region, the investigation was confined to patterns of bilingual development. That is, the differences identified may have been much greater in multilingual contexts where the variation was affected by different degrees of language use. It is in these contexts that immigrant children's performance risks being devalued since they are expected to learn school contents in a language that they are rarely exposed to outside school.

The aforementioned scenario of South Tyrol (Italy) has been analysed in another study by De Angelis (2014) with a focus on the connection between patterns of language exposure within the community and immigrants' performance on standardised tests (INVALSI). It is interesting to note that regional differences were a factor under investigation as the three languages spoken were not evenly distributed, i.e. German speakers represented the most widespread group (69%), followed by Italian speakers (26%) and then the Ladin-speaking group (4%). The results of the INVALSI (2010) standardised tests across the country revealed a significant difference in performance between first- and second-generation immigrants at the national level. Surprisingly, the same difference was not recorded in South Tyrol. Students born and raised in South Tyrol were expected to perform better compared with more recent immigrants and these results started to raise the concerns of the education board. The remedial strategies, in these cases, would have been to introduce expensive and time-consuming measures to support immigrant students to reach the same level of proficiency in the official language.

However, the study highlights that it was necessary to interpret the results of the standardised tests together with the multilingual sociolinguistic contexts where the schools were based. That is, the author provided evidence that separating the results of the standardised INVALSI tests from the local language information does not reveal reliable information to support and enhance the education systems of students coming from diverse sociolinguistic backgrounds. Hence, interpreting the results based on the students' individual linguistic profiles allows us to obtain a more complete and fair assessment since minority language speakers are compared with speakers of similar profiles instead of monolinguals or bilinguals. The contexts of acquisition as well as the type and amount of input that students receive in each language mastered is a fundamental aspect that teachers must consider in order to conceptualise the design and interpretation of assessment tools according to students' language background and living environment.

5.3 Assessing Multilinguals: The Language Experience and Proficiency Questionnaire

The Language Experience and Proficiency Questionnaire (LEAP-Q) is a self-report measure developed by Marian et al. (2007) to record the language background of speakers of multiple languages. It is considered a reliable and valid tool for constructing informative multilingual profiles and assessing language proficiency. Although the use of self-report questionnaires has been criticised within the research field, an investigation into the validity of the LEAP-Q has revealed results which suggest that self-report measures, in this case, are indicative of bilingual performance on standardised linguistic tests (Marian et al., 2007). The internal validity of the assessment has been established and replicated, suggesting that the LEAP-Q may be used as an efficient and reliable measure of bilingual language status. Specifically, the internal validity of the LEAP-Q was established on the basis of self-reported data from 52 adult multilinguals. The second study assessed the criterion-based validity on the basis of standardised language tests and self-reported measures of 50 Spanish–English bilinguals. The participants were all healthy adults with high school education or higher. The results allow the claim that the

LEAP-Q is a reliable, valid and effective tool for assessing the language profile of adult bilinguals in experimental settings. The internal validity was proved via factor analyses revealing consistent factors across both studies. On the other hand, multiple regression and correlation analyses established criterion-based validity and suggested that self-reports were reliable indicators of language performance.

The language background questionnaire is particularly suitable to assess the heterogeneous profiles of multilinguals since it includes information on the participants' level of proficiency in multiple languages (in speaking, reading, listening and writing skills), age of acquisition of each language, number and type of languages known, language choices and the amount of exposure to the languages in both a formal environment and a bilingual informal setting. Hence, it is an effective tool to test participants in all the languages they know, how they have learned them and under what circumstances. Moreover, it is a quick and effective way to obtain a large amount of information in a relatively short amount of time, only focusing on the parts of the language learning history relevant for the specific purpose of the research.

The age of acquisition of each language has been proved to be closely related to language learning, to influence participants' own perception and assessment of language proficiency and dominance and to predict their performance on behavioural tasks. The LEAP-Q elicited four age of acquisition measures for each language mastered, i.e. age of initial language learning, age of attained fluency, age of initial reading and age of attained reading fluency. Moreover, as previously discussed, the environment in which the language is learned is particularly relevant because it affects proficiency in test results. It has been argued (Flege *et al.*, 2002) that the years of formal education received in an L2 country, the years of residence in an L2 country, the average use of L1–L2 and the chronological age of acquisition of each language all affect bilingual language dominance. Accordingly, the LEAP-Q provides descriptions of acquisition modes in terms of the learning environment and in terms of the extent to which these learning environments contributed to language acquisition. Importantly, given the evidence that prior language exposure influences bilingual performance, the LEAP-Q assesses exposure to a language in four different environments, i.e. in a country, at school, at work and at home. Specifically, it elicits information about bilinguals' current exposure to each language while reading, watching TV, listening to the radio, as well as through self-instruction and language tapes.

5.4 Multilingual Teachers and Plurilingual Approaches

As already argued (see Chapter 3), one of the main factors that works as a facilitator in additional language learning is MLA because it allows learners to objectify languages as abstract systems and observe and manipulate them as objects. On the other hand, if we shift the focus from learners to teachers' plurilingual awareness, we notice that it is broader and defined as 'the complex ability to promote plurilingual approaches in the language classroom' (Otwinowska-Kasztelanic, 2014: 103). It includes, first, crosslinguistic and metalinguistic awareness of similarities and differences between the language(s) object of study. Second, knowledge about adopting the plurilingual approach in the classroom, that is enhancing learning strategies allowing students to observe similar patterns across all the languages they know. Third, it also involves a psycholinguistic awareness of individual learners' differences that facilitates the learning process such as acknowledging that bilinguals and multilinguals differ in many aspects regarding the language learning process.

All the studies reviewed and discussed in the present work, on the development of MLA and on the benefits of prior language knowledge on additional language learning, were focused on the multilingual learner. Only a few studies have included the MLA of teachers, the impact it has on language education and the best strategies available to support language teachers. The research on multilingual learners indicates that they have higher plurilingual and metalinguistic awareness than their bilingual and monolingual counterparts (Kucukali, 2021). For instance, it has been argued that multilingual teachers of English as an L2 in Australia are more likely to adopt crosslinguistic practices in their classrooms, such as using other languages to understand the target language at different levels, from phonology to pragmatics (Ellis, 2013). On the other hand, some scholars have noticed a tendency in European contexts to not exploit all the plurilingual strategies available despite the positive attitude towards plurilingual approaches (Göbel & Vieluf, 2014; Griva *et al.*, 2016).

For instance, a study conducted in Norway by Burner and Carlsen (2019) using mixed methods indicates that students' multilingual backgrounds are not used as resources in the classroom. In particular, the study investigated teachers' qualifications, perceptions and practices concerning multilingualism at a secondary school in Norway with a focus on newly arrived students. It was reported that teachers possess some basic knowledge of multilingualism, but fail to apply the knowledge in classroom settings. The main object of study was the development of students' L2, i.e. Norwegian, even in L3 classes such as English, indicating that they believe language learning occurs stepwise rather than simultaneously. However, more classroom research is needed to better understand how newly arrived students' language proficiencies are recognised, assessed, seen as resources and utilised in their education.

Hence, it can be argued that teachers do consider plurilingual approaches valuable but make little use of plurilingual strategies in multilingual teaching classes. However, it has been reported (Aronin & O'Laoire, 2004) that in third language acquisition (TLA) multilingual students prefer their teachers to exploit all the multilingual resources in the classroom to facilitate the understanding and learning process.

An interesting study conducted in Turkish contexts (Kucukali, 2021) focused on multilingual teachers, plurilingual approaches and learners' response and attitude to multilingual teachers teaching a foreign language in TLA contexts. Teachers reported using plurilingual practices in the classroom. In particular, they claimed to use at least three languages, comparing and contrasting them to teach the target language. When asked about the frequency of use, most of them answered that they implemented the strategies intuitively, whenever appropriate during the lessons. All participants displayed a positive attitude towards the use of plurilingual practices represented by two codes, namely 'facilitating effect' and 'autonomous learner'. The teachers' perspective suggests that students may benefit emotionally and mentally from plurilingual approaches. They claim that students look happier and more motivated since they can see and exploit the similarities across languages. Teachers also point out that students remember and understand better through interesting crosslinguistic examples.

In addition, the other main benefit highlighted by the study is the increased level of autonomy noticed in students who adopt and develop crosslinguistic learning strategies. Teachers reported that students started to make associations across similar languages and guess cognates by themselves:

> After a couple of explicit examples and comparisons between both languages, English and German, students are trying to find out some other similarities by themselves. This attitude could be perhaps a sign of raising awareness. (Kucukali, 2021: 80)

The most common plurilingual strategy employed by students is the use of cognates from their foreign language repertoire. As Otwinowska-Kasztelanic (2011) observes, developing awareness of cognate words and expressions may facilitate vocabulary acquisition by triggering positive transfer from the learners' L1. However, access to this lexicon depends on the psychotypological distance between the learner's L1, L2 and Ln, the number of languages known and the learner's vocabulary learning strategies. Moreover, all students used English as a bridge with other European languages including German, Russian and Spanish. Another interesting finding from this research concerns students' attitude to multilingual teachers. They all appreciated their teachers' multilingualism and associated it with diverse knowledge and higher skills. However, when they were asked to compare multilingual, bilingual and monolingual teachers, their perceptions differed. The author explains these findings in terms of both benefits and potential issues related to multilingual teachers in TLA contexts.

On the one hand, teachers expressed the view that multilingual teachers may better understand the needs of multilingual students whereas monolingual and bilingual teachers may have communication problems. On the other hand, students' data show that some monolingual and bilingual students are concerned with the difficulties that may arise from not understanding all the languages of multilingual teachers. The discrepancy of the data has been interpreted resorting to the different levels of MLA, the general proficiency in multiple languages and, consequently, the different learning strategies preferred. Another possible interpretation concerns the teachers' type of multilingualism, i.e. active bilingual or foreign language user, which explains students' preference for multilingual teachers.

What is worth observing about the study is that it represents one of the few recent works focusing on both teachers' and students' perspectives on plurilingual approaches. The findings are in line with the holistic approach to multilingualism and, moreover, they stress the cognitive and linguistic differences of multilingual learners compared with L2 learners. Hence, it offers a useful insight into the challenges of learning and teaching third or additional languages from a dual perspective. Indeed, to develop appropriate research and teaching methods to deal with multilingual learners, more studies depicting the real needs and issues of both students and teachers are needed to have a broader and inclusive portrait of multilingual classroom contexts.

5.5 Training Multilingual Teachers

An interesting contribution by Barnes and Almgren (2021) deals with training multilingual teachers in the complex linguistic background of the Basque Autonomous Community (BAC). Spanish is the home language for most children but many parents choose Basque as the language of instruction at pre-school and primary levels. This means that Basque is mainly acquired through immersion programmes. The authors looked at the knowledge acquired on language acquisition in multilingual contexts within the teacher training programme at Mondragon University. The training programme aimed to provide future pre-school and primary teachers with solid knowledge on language acquisition in bilingual and multilingual contexts. The main focus of the programme was to make future teachers aware of the type of instruments available and most suitable for the assessment of children's language development in multilingual contexts. They were asked to develop a team project, presented in English, illustrating data collected on children's linguistic portrait and considerations of their own linguistic skills and their utility in terms of multilingual education. The teaching modules delivered in English as an L3 include education and good practice in Europe and the global world; learning and teaching of L2s in multilingual context; and life place learning.

All reports reflected that the trainees were conscious of how crucial the amount of input in different languages is for children's linguistic development. Moreover, the findings conveyed a general sense of satisfaction concerning the higher degree of MLA developed and the positive attitudes and emotions towards their English language proficiency. Another interesting result relates to the attitude towards teaching. Many trainee teachers maintained that the contact with children through the project was an important occasion to become aware of appropriate teacher intervention strategies, language strategies and other strategies to develop in future according to the learners' age. In particular, one of the participants pointed out:

> To achieve good language learning and a good language development, it is important to know the children every day and work with their parents coherently. What is more, the teacher has to take different strategies such as: speak in whole sentences, establish day care routine, permit to children to listen to adult conversations, use the vocabulary that are used every day. (Barnes & Almgren, 2021: 132)

Another fundamental aspect highlighted from the study report concerns the awareness of children's anxiety and the need for appropriate approaches. Trainees observed that it is important to speak clearly, make eye contact with children and make them feel comfortable.

The authors of the study concluded that the trainee teachers' repertoire, which included Basque, Spanish and English, permits them to make instrumental use of all three languages for educational purposes. They were able to use their linguistic competence in English as an L3 to write clear reports and to make their oral presentation. These results are in line with the aforementioned 'multicompetence' concept expressed by Aronin (2016) since the aim of the task was not to evaluate native-like competence in L3 English. Instead, the study aimed at making trainee teachers understand how important their English L3 is to present and transmit the knowledge acquired. In addition, they were satisfied that they were able to handle the instruments used for evaluating language development and interpreting learners' feelings and reactions.

On the crucial role of teacher training projects in multilingual educational contexts, it is worth reporting a comparative study by Raud and Orehhova (2020) examining the content of teacher education curricula provided by European multilingual universities in Austria, Germany, Estonia, Italy, Slovakia and Slovenia. The main focus was to investigate the key components of primary teacher education curricula for multilingual schools in line with the EU guidelines on teacher training for multilingual schools. The main findings reveal that to teach in a multilingual European school, it is essential for teachers to develop knowledge of intercultural and multilingual education and skills. Moreover, teachers are also seen as personal examples of multilingualism by speaking their mother tongue, the local L2 or the language of the neighbouring state, and the English language. The importance of competence-based language and culture-sensitive teaching strategies, knowledge of how to integrate all languages of the classroom and how to integrate subject and language learning, represents the main focus of European projects supported by the European Centre for Modern Languages (2017).

5.6 Teachers as 'Knowledge Generators': Crosslinguistic and Identity Practices

In a recent work, Cummins (2021) refers to teachers as 'knowledge generators' in multilingual contexts as, through their instructional practices, they assess the usefulness and validity of the theoretical works advanced by scholars in the field of multilingualism. In particular, teachers contribute to the generation of theories connecting instruction to students' lives. Indeed, if the role of researchers is to analyse logical coherence of theoretical assumptions in the field of education, the criteria of empirical adequacy and logical coherence are incomplete by themselves. That is, the effectiveness of educational theories in the field of multilingual education can only be confirmed or rejected by a dialogue between theory, research, policy and practice.

The author examines and reports on a number of multilingual instructional projects implementing translanguaging and crosslinguistic transfer approaches to demonstrate how powerful the impact of the collaboration between researchers and teachers can be. Specifically, Cummins (2014) refers to four categories of teaching 'through a multilingual lens', varying in terms of complexity from simple activities to more elaborate projects belonging to the translanguaging/identity texts landscape. That is, 'these projects extend the classroom instructional space to enable students to engage in creative writing and artistic endeavours that express and affirm their emerging academic and personal identities' (Cummins, 2021: 313). The four practices include:

- Simple everyday practices to make students' languages visible and audible within the school.
- Encouraging students to use their home languages for typical school activities such as reading, research and note-taking.
- Using technology in creative ways to build awareness of language, geography and intercultural realities.
- Dual language project work.

In regard to the simple everyday practices, they can be easily implemented in any school context involving multilingual learners and convey a symbolic value of inclusion and representation of heritage language speakers together with their own identities. Among the most important practices listed, it is worth mentioning learning greetings in all the languages of the classroom, displaying students' works in both the school and home language within the school spaces, providing multilingual versions of the school signs and bringing a word or phrase in the home language into the classroom every day and explaining the meaning. The benefits of implementing these multilingual instructional activities go beyond the development of multilingual awareness in multiple languages. The inclusion of different languages within the classroom leads to positive attitudes towards other cultures and develops a wider geographical awareness of the places of origin of multilingual students. Moreover, the promotion of students' linguistic and cultural backgrounds represents a process of negotiating identities.

The second practice propounded is the use of home languages for reading, research, note-taking and other academic work. For instance, teachers encourage new students with a different L1 to access, through the internet, home language resources to better understand their background knowledge of the teaching contents. Also, teachers can encourage newcomers and bilingual students to use their home language to develop projects to present to the whole classroom. In this way, even students with limited knowledge of the school language can still carry out the project. Moreover, school libraries should be equipped with home language and dual language books for students. The school could also work with parents to set up a home language book exchange where it is possible to donate home language books that children have finished reading. Apart from providing additional multilingual material for the school, this initiative encourages fruitful collaboration between teachers and parents and conveys the importance of reading to children in their home languages to enhance biliteracy and bilingualism. In social studies, at high school levels, it is suggested to encourage students to research material in their home languages. Ted Talks, for instance, are available with subtitles in more than 100 languages and represent a useful tool to discuss topics easily understood and shared by all classroom members. In addition, teachers can establish relationships with community members, inviting them to share their stories in the school language or in the community language with a translation provided.

Another instructional practice deals with the use of technology in creative ways to build awareness of language, geography and intercultural realities. For instance, an efficient practice involves the use of Google Translate or other free translation resources to translate a story written in the students' home language. The translation obtained is a rough version of the text in the school language to be understood by teachers and the other students. In the second phase, the teacher works on the obtained translation with the newcomer student to edit the text and create an acceptable version in the school language. On the other hand,

Google Earth can be used to access the countries of origin of the students to compare aspects of their countries of origin to the social, geographical and climate realities of their new countries. It can also be exploited as a source to develop historical awareness of the main events at particular stages in history. In science, the effects of climate change, for example, could be compared between the country of origin and the new country.

Finally, among the dual language project work practices in multilingual contexts reported by Cummins (2021), it is worth recalling the creation of dual language books or curriculum-related projects by means of programmes such as PowerPoint. Also, students can be encouraged to express their ideas and insights through poetry (or other genres of writing) in both their home and school language. They could start writing in the language they feel more confident with and translate the text into the other language, also involving other students who share the same linguistic repertoire. A study by Jiménez et al. (2015), for instance, with Spanish/English bilingual participants, conveyed the benefits of crosslinguistic translation to provide opportunities to deepen their awareness of language and understanding of texts from considering all the linguistic levels, from lexicon to semantics. On the one hand, these projects aimed at enhancing the multilingual repertoire of students by softening the boundaries among the different languages known in multilingual practices. On the other hand, importantly, by making all the languages visible and acknowledged in the classroom through crosslinguistic and cross-cultural references, the projects emphasised and valued the heterogeneous identities of multilingual learners as a precious resource to exploit.

An important aspect to highlight about the examples taken from the four types of crosslinguistic and identity projects in multilingual classrooms is that they are all rather easy to implement and they do not require any expensive or radical changes to the education system. As discussed in Chapter 4, translanguaging theories have had a considerable impact on the development of multilingual pedagogical practices worldwide. Nonetheless, before proceeding to the analysis of different contributions to translanguaging literature developed in different multilingual areas with a significant number of immigrant students, it is worth looking at some examples of crosslinguistic instruction. They provide a useful tool to better understand the passage from pedagogies characterised by linguistic separation, first, to the integration of different languages, in a second phase, and the conception of languages with fluid or non-existing boundaries.

An early example of crosslinguistic instruction in European contexts is represented by a plurilingual pedagogy project carried out by an Irish school in the western suburbs of Dublin over a period of 20 years (Little & Kirwin, 2019; Kirwin, 2020). The pedagogical orientation was characterised by five principles, i.e. an inclusive ethos, an open language policy and an integrated approach to language education, a strong emphasis on the development of literary skills, teaching methods that strive to be as explicit as possible and respect for teachers' professional autonomy. After examining different examples of how the pedagogical principles were implemented with the enthusiasm of both teachers and pupils, the authors emphasised several benefits.

In particular, the most interesting aspect recorded is that, despite the presence of a considerable number of immigrants with a lower socio-economic background, the school's standardised test scores in English and mathematics have been at or above the national average. This is in contrast with the underachievement of most schools within European countries, particularly in those contexts with about 25% of immigrant learners. The most interesting implications of the research by Little and Kirwin (2019), as cited by Cummins (2021: 328), are that 'encouraging immigrant-background learners to use their home languages inside and outside the school promotes crosslinguistic comparisons and development of language awareness, both of which contribute to pupils' educational success'.

Another contribution exemplifying crosslinguistic instructional practices in Europe comes from a project carried out in France by Hélot and Young (2006), which shows the effects of a language awareness model. The project, initiated by elementary school teachers in 2000, aimed to sensitise students to the wide variety of languages and cultures spoken by students and their teachers in the school. It represents an important example of teachers considered as knowledge generators since they invited parents to share aspects of their languages and cultures with schoolchildren aged between six and nine during Saturday morning sessions. This initiative involved the exposure to 18 different languages and cultures and, most importantly, highlighted the importance of the collaboration between teachers and parents. Among the range of awareness activities propounded, the authors included singing, cooking, learning geography, histories of migration, listening to develop phonological awareness and feeling respect for languages spoken by other members of the class. Reporting the comments of a teacher on the experience of Turkish background children with their family members involved in the project, the authors stressed the impact of the language and culture awareness initiatives to affirm the identities of minority students and communities. For example, a teacher pointed out: 'Now they exist in the class, before they did not even exist' (Hélot & Young, 2006: 80). As a matter of fact, they started to participate more actively in class activities and acknowledged the acceptance of their home language together with French.

Other interesting examples of crosslinguistic projects were implemented in Canada between the late 1990s and 2000s. Particularly, the Dual Language Showcase (Schecter & Cummins, 2003), implemented by Grade 1 teacher Chow at Thornwood Public School in Toronto, was the first Canadian project implemented by teachers to involve students' linguistic repertoire for instructional purposes even though the teachers did not speak these languages. In addition, the project also focused on the impact that publishing classroom dual language stories has on student identity. The main aim of the project was to examine the effectiveness of pedagogical practices to be implemented in multilingual and multicultural contexts. The role of the teacher who ideated the project was crucial in engaging students and their parents in literacy activities, i.e. writing stories in their L1 and translating them in English.

Over the course of 15 years, dual language texts in multiple languages were posted on the school's website. Newcomer students with a lower proficiency in English started to write in their home language or developed the text in English and afterwards, supported by teachers and parents who mastered their home language, translated it into their L1. The Dual Language Show had a considerable impact on the Ministry of Education and school policymakers by demonstrating that teachers have the potential to include multiple languages in the instructional context, engaging students' and parents' multilingual resources even when these languages were unknown to teachers.

Patricia Chow, of Chinese descent, was in a position to share her knowledge of Chinese and French with students and, most importantly, she conveyed interest in and curiosity towards other languages and cultures through numerous simple everyday activities. For instance, she asked students to share their knowledge of other languages when singing, greeting, counting, etc. She maintained that:

> Students love to see their languages displayed in this way and understand that their languages are acknowledged and valued in the classroom. They are therefore not inhibited in displaying their knowledge of additional languages and take pride in their linguistic expertise. (Chow & Cummins, 2003: 46–47)

Hence, again, the most important concern is to make students' languages visible, valued and appreciated in the classroom. Their multilingual and multicultural repertoire is an essential part of additional language learning. It is seen as a fundamental resource to exploit to enhance TLA.

5.7 Translanguaging: The Teachers' Perspective

As already mentioned, translanguaging was mainly introduced as a practice to teach bilingual students in Wales. Accordingly, Welsh scholars have been studying ways to develop this practice as a pedagogy. In particular, Williams (2012) distinguishes between natural and official translanguaging. The first refers to all those acts and strategies employed by students to learn, but it includes teachers' use of translanguaging, the focus of this chapter, to make sure that contents and meanings are properly conveyed. On the other hand, official translanguaging is mainly conducted by teachers but it can also be employed by students, as argued by Williams (2012: 39). Specifically, it is used by teachers orally to explain a term relating to a particular subject or a general term and to explain complex parts of the topic being taught. In writing, it is used by teachers when short translations are required. In Williams' view, students make use of translanguaging to explain something in another language to show full understanding of the subject area; to talk to parents who do not understand the language; and in tests and examinations when they find it difficult to convey the exact information in the other language.

According to Lewis *et al.* (2012b), there is a fundamental difference between teacher-directed translanguaging and the previously described translanguaging employed by learners (see Chapter 4). Teacher-directed translanguaging involves planned and structured activities by the teacher and is conceived as a transformative pedagogy. To meet the needs of learners' diverse profiles in a classroom, from a linguistic, social, educational and experiential point of view, teachers are required to act holistically and to differentiate instruction. In this way, all learners can receive appropriate linguistic input, produce the right output and be cognitively involved. Particularly for emergent bilinguals, teachers make use of translanguaging approaches as scaffolding to ensure that the learners are able to deal with difficult contents and texts, and produce new language practice and knowledge. It is also a transformative pedagogy, allowing us to overcome the binary logics and sustain bilingual identities. The role of teachers changes completely since they abandon their authority role in the classroom to embrace one that leads them to facilitate project-based instruction and collaborative grouping to maximise translanguaging.

Busch (2011) maintains that to adopt translanguaging for teaching requires a 'critical gesture' of language practices that aims at developing a high degree of linguistic awareness. Precisely, teachers' translanguaging is focused on language practice as a resource but it also includes students' discourses, concerns and topics. Most importantly, a teacher who uses translanguaging participates in the process as a learner, adopting a multivoicedness. For minority language students, as has been argued, it is particularly important to build on students' linguistic strengths and to reduce the risks of alienation since it involves linguistic and cultural references familiar to them.

A practical example of translanguaging practice, developed by Kano (2010), enabled Japanese students to become more aware of the differences between Japanese and English from a structural point of view, to produce better English essays. In particular, her translanguaging approach followed three main steps:

(1) Students read bilingual texts on the topic of the assignment, presented either side by side or there was an English text coupled with a parallel translation in Japanese.
(2) Students discussed the bilingual readings mostly in Japanese.
(3) Students produced essays in English on the topic of the bilingual reading and the discussion in Japanese.

Since this practice leads students to move back and forth along the continuum of their whole multilingual repertoire, overcoming the strict boundaries between languages, one of the features enhanced was greater linguistic awareness. That is to say, their written production in English was linguistically enriched by the attention paid to their Japanese language and cultural practices.

García *et al.* (2012) have reported the use of translanguaging by teachers working in New York schools with emergent bilingual students. The three main metafunctions identified are:

(1) conceptualisation of key words and elements;
(2) development of MLA;
(3) creation of affective bonds with students.

On the other hand, in Michael-Luna and Canagarajah's (2007) words, translanguaging practices are described as code-meshing strategies. They include selecting multilingual texts, that is including texts in different languages to activate prior linguistic knowledge; modelling oral and written code-meshing to encourage student agency in language choice; and scaffolding the negotiation with the text.

An interesting example of an analysis of language use by teachers and students comes from a recent study by Muguruza *et al.* (2020). In a university in the Basque country, the authors examined students' reaction to the flexible use of three languages as a medium of instruction: English, Basque, and Spanish. The syllabus of the course 'Language Planning: Social and Educational Perspectives', addressed to second- and third-year students of social education, explains that it is an English medium instruction (EMI) course with a flexible language policy. 'The materials and lectures are in English but you are free to use English, Basque, and Spanish to take part in the class and to complete your work'. The purpose of the language policy is to reduce comprehension problems due to the EMI. It is based on a translanguaging approach described by Canagarajah (2011: 401) in these terms: 'the ability of multilingual speakers to shuttle between languages, treating the diverse languages that form their repertoire as an integrated system'.

The findings of the study show that the flexible use of languages by teachers and students helped students to feel free to communicate their meanings and interact choosing among three languages. Translanguaging made it easier for them to follow the course and a lower level of anxiety was reported compared to a course only taught in English. Finally, it has been observed that even though students reacted positively to the flexible use of languages proposed by the teacher, this policy does not encourage the use of English for production. The percentage of English use in classroom interaction and in written texts was very limited, suggesting that there is room for improvement in English production skills. Nonetheless, the policy allowed students to attend a course partly taught in English despite their limited proficiency level. Indeed, the results of the Oxford Placement Text highlighted a significant increase in their level of English, which was explained by the fact that translanguaging supported them in the development of general comprehension skills.

Thus, what can be noticed from the examples reported and discussed is that teachers use translanguaging to support students during the acquisition phase, although considering the nation-state school language and the child's language as separate identities. García and Li (2015), in particular, identify seven purposes of translanguaging as used by teachers:

(1) to differentiate among students' levels and adapt instruction to different types of students in multilingual classrooms (i.e. monolinguals, bilinguals, emergent bilinguals);
(2) to build background knowledge so that students can make meaning of the content object of study;
(3) to deepen understandings and cognitive engagement, develop and extend new knowledge and develop critical thinking;
(4) to enhance crosslinguistic transfer and MLA to strengthen the students' ability to translanguage in order to meet the communicative needs of a particular sociocultural context;
(5) for crosslinguistic flexibility;
(6) for identity investment and positionality, to engage learners;
(7) to interrogate linguistic inequality and disrupt sociopolitical structures to engage in social justice.

Hence, from the point of view of teachers, translanguaging can be seen as a fruitful instrument to support multilingual learners' process of TLA; as an inclusive practice to overcome linguistic and cultural barriers in the classroom; and to reinforce the multicultural identity of learners by building a bridge between school and community.

5.8 Inspiring Instructional Practices

Translanguaging strategies have been grouped into three main categories. First, teacher attentiveness to meaning making by translanguaging to favour understanding and to encourage inner speech. Second, teacher use of classroom resources for translanguaging which include the design of multilingual and multimodal texts and technologically enhanced media, multilingual and multimodal classroom landscape such as listening and visual texts, technologically enhanced media, multilingual word walls, multilingual sentence starters and cognate walls. Third, teacher design of classroom and curricular structures for translanguaging including peer grouping according to home language to enable collaborative dialogue and cooperative tasks; project and task-based learning to build on multimedia and kinetics; research tasks; and language inquiry tasks to build translanguage capacities and extend MLA to all levels of the linguistic system.

In Chapter 4, the impact of translanguaging theories and practices was discussed from a theoretical point of view and from the students' perspective. The current section is focused on the implementation of those practices from the point of view of teachers working with students of multilingual and multicultural backgrounds in different geographical areas. One of the most comprehensive examples of research on translanguaging comes from a study carried out in Italy by Carbonara and Scibetta (2020a, 2020b) focused on the analysis of classroom interaction and students' work in five different schools. The 'AltRoparlante' project collected data based on the observation of teachers' instruction, parents' questionnaires and multiple interviews with teachers and students stressing the importance of collaboration between research and education. In the initial phase, researchers encouraged teachers to communicate their instructional strategies and techniques based on translanguaging during monthly meetings where activities were planned, reported and discussed. Moreover, the project team guided teachers in the data collection focused on the linguistic repertoires of students and their families to raise awareness of how students use their languages in different contexts. Also, it allowed researchers to build a constructive dialogue with teachers to better examine students' attitudes and perceptions towards other languages and how to acknowledge the legitimacy of multiple languages in the school context.

After the initial implementing phase, teachers started to work alone to explore the translanguaging instructional possibilities with their students with oral, written and other subject content activities. With older students, the instructional practices were more explicitly focused on issues including language rights and social inequalities to develop critical thinking of how power relations affect our society. Among the positive aspects that emerged from the study, the authors focused on students' MLA, academic engagement and attitudes towards multilingualism and their home languages. In particular, they argued that 'Immigrant minority languages, usually confined to a minoritised position, began to be convinced by student as educational resources for learning and meaning-making' (Carbonara & Scibetta, 2020b: 17).

The most important finding that emerged from the study concerns the acknowledgement by teachers that the multilingual and multicultural repertoire of students can be employed as an effective instructional tool to give voice to the minority languages and cultures of the community. Moreover, it has been argued (Cummins, 2021: 342) that it is a way to challenge the aforementioned societal power relations that 'stigmatise community talents and identities'. Hence, these practices allow teachers and students, both monolinguals and bilinguals, to rebuild their roles and identities. Teachers in these projects become aware that to teach the dominant language and engage all students in the school activities is to acknowledge and appreciate the language and cultural diversity of students, making them feel like a precious resource, together with their diverse linguistic, cultural and knowledge background. This means starting to bring their own experiences as multilinguals within the school practices.

Another notable contribution to the translanguaging literature is the research conducted by Mary and Young (2017, 2021), who analysed the effects of the instructional practices undertaken by one pre-school teacher in the Alsace region of France. The study shows that the role of teachers in transforming the educational experience of minoritised students is of paramount importance. The authors collected data consisting of video-recorded interactions and activities involving Sylvie, a pre-school teacher working with children from a low socioeconomic background in the northeast of France, pupils and their families. Sylvie's pedagogical approach rejected the assimilationist practices leading the French education system. Indeed, over her 30 years career with minority language students, she learned basic words and expressions in their languages, interacting with them and with their parents. She used her limited proficiency in multiple languages to facilitate children's learning. Different from other colleagues, Sylvie encouraged the use of students' home languages to tell stories and comment on books, inviting parents to actively participate in the classroom's activities.

Mary and Young (2017) define four main goals characterising the teacher's translanguaging practices: meeting children's basic needs; making connections between home and school; building on children's prior knowledge and scaffolding their learning of French; and fostering engagement with literacy. What particularly emerges from Sylvie's translanguaging classroom practices are her beliefs and ideologies about language and language use, her commitment to social equality, her commitment to challenge the prevailing monolingual bias and norms in education and being aware of the social role played by languages. Hence, to use Cummin's words, Sylvie's educational practices represent an example of 'teachers as knowledge generators'. She tried to engage children's multilingual repertoire to scaffold instruction and to give voice to minority students' languages and cultures. In other words, she aimed at bridging the gap between instruction and children's lives outside school.

Another contribution taking into account the point of view of teachers in the implementation of translanguaging practices is the research conducted by Martinez-García and Arnold (2020). It discusses the work carried out in a university master's course in Dallas (Texas) which focused on the improvement of the teaching methods of instructors of Spanish as a foreign language, involving different educational backgrounds and levels. The authors provide concrete examples of how to approach multilingual classrooms by outlining the translanguaging techniques employed by students and teachers. The real example materials of the study included multimodal teaching tools in different languages and referring to different countries. Moreover, all the original texts were supported by a translation in Spanish, the official language of instruction.

The most important finding of the study is the teachers' understanding of students' languages and background as a mechanism to help them better grasp the content of the classroom. Indeed, understanding students' linguistic background means identifying their native languages, the languages they have studied and the level of proficiency reached in each language. This is of paramount importance in choosing the didactic material suitable for the class. In particular, students were divided into different groups and were asked to experience the techniques themselves, pretending to be real students of a foreign language. Two main strategies related to their language background were employed to make sure that students could benefit from the demonstrations. First, examples of pieces of literature in languages different from the vernacular language of the classroom were included. Second, the length and complexity of the selected texts varied according to the proficiency level of the different groups. Matching the selected material to the students' ability allowed all students enough time to understand and discuss the text. Most importantly, not only did these strategies engage all students but they were also a successful tool to create meaningful experiences including students at the high-achieving level.

Another crucial aspect conveyed by this research is the focus on 'making use of students' needs in the learning process'. In the specific field of translanguaging, this concept has been interpreted as 'making sure that students approach each new topic by thinking how to apply it to their own future needs' (Martinez-García & Arnold, 2020: 42). In other words, instructors have the role of designing class materials making sure that students are aware that they can apply the same knowledge differently according to their needs. For instance, an interesting technique used by the instructor of the course when faced with this challenge was to engage students at the end of the lesson in brainstorming activities aimed at pinpointing different contexts of application of what they had just learned. Hence, once again, translanguaging strategies are not limited to understanding and assessing students' linguistic abilities, but are also aimed at understanding and integrating their diverse personal experiences and backgrounds, creating a diverse and multiculturally engaging classroom setting. The specific aspect that deserves attention is the focus on the instructor's role as a guide and monitor for students to understand how to use their own 'translanguaging mechanism' to better exploit the content conveyed in the classroom.

5.9 Conclusion

The examples of instructional practices based on crosslinguistic, identity and translanguaging theories discussed in this chapter represent a practical and inspiring tool for teachers working with students from multicultural and multilingual backgrounds. They constitute a practical application of the theoretical framework outlined in the previous chapters, and of the effective pedagogical theories to be implemented in multilingual education. What is worth noting from a teacher's perspective is the need to create a fruitful and inclusive space where all the different languages and cultures of the students are considered as a precious resource to exploit and to develop for additional language learning. Students' multilingual repertoire can also work as scaffolding for students' access to instruction in the dominant school language.

In addition, by merging different representations, histories and backgrounds, translanguaging has the potential to break the monolingual bias in education and the standard language ideal to achieve via schooling. Indeed, translanguaging practices support and include those speakers of minority languages who are often stigmatised and excluded from educational programmes. It has the potential to develop more sophisticated discourse, deeper comprehension of multilingual texts, the production of complex texts, the evaluation and enhancement of prior linguistic and cultural knowledge and, most importantly, the inclusion of all learners' voices, as endorsed by teachers and educators first.

Finally, the educational practices compared and discussed suggest the importance of merging pedagogical theories and instructional practices. Indeed, the collaboration between researchers and teachers, i.e. action research, is paramount in the development and implementation of multilingual instruction. Researchers, on the one hand, offer a useful guide to teachers and educators propounding different theories to be applied in instructional settings based on students' multilingual and multicultural repertoire. On the other hand, teachers play a fundamental role in educational research advancement, observing the learning strategies of multilingual learners when dealing with metalinguistic tasks. Indeed, teachers must be properly trained to face the challenges of teaching in multilingual and multicultural contexts. On the other hand, the challenges faced by multilingual students when dealing with additional languages can only be thoroughly understood through a comprehensive analysis provided by all three practices outlined in this chapter, i.e. multilingual teaching, testing and assessing. Indeed, the complex and unique cognitive and linguistic profile of multilingual learners cannot be considered just as a quantitative matter. Multilinguals cannot be compared to the sum of several monolinguals since the qualitative difference reflects their specific language processing, learning strategies and communicative needs.

Nonetheless, although translanguaging has been considered an effective practical theory of languages to fully exploit the multilingual and multicultural repertoire and give voice to minority language students, it is crucial to point out that it is not the only solution available. The dangers of seeing translanguaging as the only instructional option is that all the other possible routes to create educational spaces embracing multilingual learners from diverse linguistic and cultural backgrounds with their unique profile, risk being overlooked. Instead, multiple approaches resulting from a never-ending dialogue between research and teaching are advisable to fully understand the challenges of multilingual teaching and learning and offer different solutions tailored to the learners' communicative needs.

Conclusion

The discussion on multilingualism included in this volume has been guided by the principle of presenting multilingual acquisition as a different process from second language acquisition (SLA) from a cognitive, linguistic, educational and affective point of view. What differs considerably between the two processes is the profile of the language learners. Hence, the most influential crosslinguistic and transfer theories and speech production models advanced in third language acquisition (TLA) are compared and contrasted to highlight how the two processes, i.e. SLA and TLA, are inherently different. Moreover, to better understand the most important speech production models currently used in research on multilingualism, Chapter 1 investigates the main characteristics of monolingual and bilingual models to explain how they were enhanced and adapted to TLA research. However, it is important to bear in mind that all the models available, tailored to portray multilingual minds, can be considered as mere adaptations of previously developed bilingual or monolingual processing models. Hence, the intent of the volume is to raise awareness about the need to develop research in the TLA area to obtain more specific and reliable tools of investigation that take into account the complex and dynamic nature of multilingualism from a holistic perspective. This would provide a more accurate representation of how multilinguals process the linguistic input and learn additional languages. In this mechanism, it is crucial to consider the role of previous languages that may, tacitly or explicitly, influence additional language learning in terms of the process itself and the outcome.

Another crucial thread of the volume, addressed in Chapter 2, is confronting the bilingual paradox. Starting from the myth of disadvantages and cognitive delay associated with bilinguals, it is then demonstrated how the methodological approach and the research aptitude towards bilingualism have changed considerably through history. If, on the one hand, from an educational perspective, the prejudices concerning bilingual disadvantages have been overcome leaving space for a positive and inclusive approach to TLA, on the other, the cognitive area of study still reflects some nuances of uncertainty when dealing with the bilingual advantage. However, after comparing and contrasting different contributions on the issue, the apparent contradictions can be resolved looking at the specific factors of investigation, more specifically, the analysis of representation and control of attention.

Additionally, an ample section of the book is dedicated to defining the factors making bilinguals better learners of additional languages. The main conclusion drawn is that what facilitates bilinguals in additional language learning is their knowledge of previous languages due to the experience gained in the language learning process, the strategies developed and the role of the transfer of lexical and morphosyntactic patterns between first language/second language (L1/L2) and third language and other (L3/Ln). The volume provides an insight into the controversial discussion on the nature and role of metalinguistic awareness (MLA) in additional language learning. It presents the non-unitary nature of MLA, which may be considered both cognitive and linguistic, implicit and explicit, examining its mediating role in TLA. Considering that MLA is complex and difficult to assess experimentally, a number of variables reported to affect its development are explored to disentangle the relationship between MLA and type of bilingualism, literacy and implicit and explicit instruction. Hence, the aim is to present the readers with a more complete portrait of the relationship between the aforementioned factors and MLA on the one hand, and MLA and performance in additional languages on the other. The relevance of each aspect is discussed in terms of multilingual educational practices.

Starting from a reflection based on how humans communicate and interact, alternating different codes and linguistic varieties, the book introduces and discusses one of the most innovative and debated linguistic theories and practices, i.e. translanguaging. It is propounded as a tool that particularly suits those educational contexts where more than two languages are involved. The principle is to exploit the multilingual and multimodal resources that constitute the repertoire of multilingual speakers and learners. The latter is considered a precious resource to exploit rather than an obstacle to overcome. Hence, a translanguaging approach allows us to go beyond the traditional and unfruitful dichotomies characterising former education systems where the native speaker competence was the idealised level of language to achieve. Translanguaging allows more dynamic and interacting alternations of codes, styles, registers and varieties of languages where the communicative functionality is the real teaching and learning objective.

Another crucial aspect highlighted about this educational approach is the empowerment of multiple cultural identities typical of multilingual classrooms where diversity becomes the key word to make the invisible visible and appreciated. The boundaries between school contexts on the one hand and community on the other become nuances since any formal and informal context where languages are used can become an important occasion to reinforce and enhance language learning. This leads to the full utilisation of all the multilingual and multisemiotic resources of learners to interact and communicate in their daily lives, inside and outside the classroom. Importantly, since this practice constructs a new multifaceted identity, translanguaging becomes an effective tool to counteract ostracism and racism towards minority language groups. It supports and includes those speakers of minority languages often stigmatised and excluded from educational programmes. Hence, the broader and fluid linguistic repertoire and the type of resources needed, available and exploited during the whole acquisition process need to be analysed and included. The learning strategies combined and used by multilingual learners for specific linguistic tasks need to be considered to thoroughly understand the specific nature of third or additional language acquisition and learning.

In the concluding chapter of the book, a shift of focus occurs from a learning to a teaching perspective. It provides different examples of instructional practices based on crosslinguistic, identity and translanguaging theories to inspire teachers and prospective teachers dealing with learners with multicultural and multilingual backgrounds. They constitute a practical application of all the theories discussed in the previous chapters to stress the importance of developing teaching practice, assessing and testing tools tailored to the language learners' profile. The leading principle is to create an inclusive space where multiple languages, identities and cultures are emphasised and valued. Students' multilingual repertoire is used as scaffolding, allowing teachers to facilitate instruction in additional languages. A more sophisticated discourse is sought to improve the comprehension of multilingual and multimodal texts and the production of complex texts. Prior knowledge of languages becomes a fundamental tool to apply the strategies and skills already developed to additional languages. Most importantly, it allows the inclusion of all learners' voices, mediated by teachers and educators.

Finally, another aspect of paramount importance is the collaboration between researchers and teachers. Not only does this approach consider teachers as knowledge generators, acknowledging their fundamental role from an educational perspective, but it also reinforces the synergic collaboration between teaching and research, enriching and enhancing multilingual teaching and helping to implement multilingual practices based on real challenges reported by teachers in multilingual contexts. Researchers provide the theoretical framework and empirical background to support teachers and educators based on the cognitive and linguistic theories developed in the field of TLA. On the other hand, teachers concretely observe the learning strategies of multilingual learners when dealing with additional languages, noticing all the aspects that are likely to enhance or delay the multilingual learning process. Hence, it is necessary that teachers receive specific training to face the challenges of teaching in multilingual and multicultural contexts. However, as argued, these challenges can only be thoroughly understood through a comprehensive analysis of multilingual teaching, testing and assessing. Indeed, the complex and unique cognitive and linguistic profile of multilingual learners cannot be reduced to a mere quantitative difference, i.e. two languages vs three or more languages. It is not the number of languages that make multilingual learners unique. The difference needs to be sought in the way they process, understand and produce messages in multiple languages, their learning strategies and their communicative needs.

References

Achugar, M. (2006) Writers on the borderlands: Constructing a bilingual identity in Southwest Texas. *Journal of Language, Identity, and Education* 5 (2), 97–122.

Adesope, O.O., Lavin, T., Thompson, T. and Ungerleider, C. (2010) A systematic review and meta-analysis of the cognitive correlates of bilingualism. *Review of Educational Research* 80 (2), 207–245.

Aldekoa, A., Manterola, I. and Idiazabal, I. (2020) A trilingual teaching sequence for oral presentation skills in Basque, Spanish and English. *The Language Learning Journal* 48, 259–271.

Antoniou, M. (2019) The advantages of bilingualism debate. *Annual Review of Linguistics* 5, 395–415.

Ardasheva, Y. and Tretter, T. (2012) Perceptions and use of language learning strategies among ESL teachers and ELLs. *TESOL Journal* 33 (3–4), 552–585.

Aronin, L. (2006) Dominant language constellations: An approach to multilingualism studies. In M. O'Laoire (ed.) *Multilingualism in Educational Settings* (pp. 140–159). Hohengehren: Schneider Publications.

Aronin, L. (2016) Multicompetence and dominant language constellation. In V. Cook and Li, W. (eds) *The Cambridge Handbook of Linguistic Multicompetence* (pp. 142–163). Cambridge: Cambridge University Press.

Aronin, L. and O'Laoire, M. (2004) Exploring multilingualism in cultural contexts: Towards a notion of multilinguality. In C. Hoffmann and J. Ytsma (eds) *Trilingualism in Family, School and Community* (pp. 11–29). Clevedon: Multilingual Matters.

Aronin, L. and Hufeisen, B. (2009) *The Exploration of Multilingualism: Development of Research on L3, Multilingualism and Multiple Language Acquisition*. Amsterdam: John Benjamins.

Baddeley, A.D. (1992) Working memory. *Science* 255 (5044), 556–559.

Baker, C. (2000) *The Care and Education of Young Bilinguals: An Introduction for Professionals*. Clevedon: Multilingual Matters.

Bardel, C. and Falk, Y. (2007) The role of the second language in third language acquisition: The case of Germanic syntax. *Second Language Research* 23 (4), 459–484.

Barnes, J. and Almgren, M. (2021) Training teachers for the challenges of multilingual education. In J. Pinto and N. Alexandre (eds) *Multilingualism and Third Language Acquisition: Learning and Teaching Trends*. Berlin: Language Science Press.

Barratt, L. (2018) Monolingual bias: Non-native English-speaking teachers. In J.I. Liontas (ed.) *The TESOL Encyclopaedia of English language teaching* (pp. 1–7). https://doi.org/10.1002/9781118784235.eelt0024.

Barratt, L. (2019) Studying language and linguistics through a plurilingual lens. *Linguistics and the Human Sciences* 13 (3), 294–315.

Bates, E. and MacWhinney, B. (1982) Functionalist approaches to grammar. In E. Wanner and L. Gleitman (eds) *Language Acquisition: The State of the Art* (pp. 173–218). Cambridge: Cambridge University Press.

Beacco, J.C., Byram, M., Cavalli, M., Coste, D., Cuenat, M.E., Goullier, F. and Panthier, J. (2010) *Guide for the Development and Implementation of Curricula for Plurilingual and Intercultural Education*. Strasbourg: Council of Europe.

Berard, T.J. (2005) Rethinking practices and structures. *Philosophy of the Social Sciences* 35 (2), 196–230.

Berthele, R. (2020) The extraordinary ordinary: Re-engineering multilingualism as a natural category. *Language Learning* 71 (1), 80–120.

Bialystok, E. (2001) *Bilingualism in Development: Language, Literacy and Cognition*. Cambridge: Cambridge University Press.

Bialystok, E. (2009) Bilingualism: The good, the bad, and the indifferent. *Bilingualism: Language and Cognition* 12 (1), 3–11.

Bialystok, E. (2020) Bilingual effects on cognition in children. In L. Zhang (ed.) *The Oxford Research Encyclopedia of Education*. Oxford: Oxford University Press. https://doi.org/10.1093/acrefore/9780190264093.013.962.

Bialystok, E. and Majumder, S. (1998) The relationship between bilingualism and the development of cognitive processes in problem solving. *Applied Psycholinguistics* 19, 69–85.

Bialystok, E. and Feng, X. (2009) Language proficiency and executive control in proactive interference: Evidence from monolingual and bilingual children and adults. *Brain and Language* 109, 93–100.

Bialystok, E. and Barac, R. (2012) Emerging bilingualism: Dissociating advantages for metalinguistic awareness and executive control. *Cognition* 122 (1), 67–73.

Blake, D. and Hanley, V. (1995) *Dictionary of Educational Terms*. Aldershot: Arena.

Blommaert, J. (2016) From mobility to complexity in sociolinguistic theory and method. In N. Coupland (ed.) *Sociolinguistics: Theoretical Debates* (pp. 242–260). Cambridge: Cambridge University Press.

Bloor, T. (1986) What do language students know about grammar? *British Journal of Language Teaching* 24, 157–160.

Bowden, H., Sanz, C. and Stafford, A. (2005) Individual differences: Age, sex, working memory, and prior knowledge. In C. Sanz (ed.) *Mind and Context in Adult Second Language Acquisition: Methods, Theory and Practice* (pp. 105–140). Washington, DC: Georgetown University Press.

Burner, T. and Carlsen, C. (2019) Teacher qualifications, perceptions and practices concerning multilingualism at a school for newly arrived students in Norway. *International Journal of Multilingualism* 19, 35–49.

Busch, B. (2011) Building on heteroglossia and heterogeneity: The experience of a multilingual classroom. Presentation at the Third International Conference on Language, Education and Diversity (LED) Colloquium; Language, Education, and Superdiversity, University of Auckland, New Zealand.

Cabrelli Amaro, J. and Rothman, J. (2010) On L3 acquisition and phonological permeability: A new test case for debates on the mental representation of non-native phonological systems. *IRAL* 48, 275–296.

Canagarajah, S. (2004) Multilingual writers and the struggle for voice in academic discourse. In A. Pavlenko and A. Blackledge (eds) *Negotiation of Identities in Multilingual Contexts* (pp. 266–289). Clevedon: Multilingual Matters.

Canagarajah, S. (2011) Translanguaging in the classroom: Emerging issues for research and pedagogy. *Applied Linguistics Review* 2, 1–28.

Canagarajah, S. (2013) *Translingual Practice: Global Englishes and Cosmopolitan Relations*. New York: Routledge.

Carbonara, V. and Scibetta, A. (2020a) Integrating translanguaging pedagogy into Italian primary schools: Implications for language practices and children's empowerment. *International Journal of Bilingual Education and Bilingualism* 25, 1049–1069.

Carbonara, V. and Scibetta, A. (2020b) *Imparare attraverso le lingue. Translanguaging come praticadidattica*. Roma: Carocci.

Carlson, S.M. and Meltzoff, A.N. (2008) Bilingual experience and executive functioning in young children. *Developmental Science* 11 (2), 282–298.

Carroll, J.B. (1981) Twenty-five years of research on foreign language aptitude. In K.C. Diller (ed.) *Individual Differences and Universals in Language Learning Aptitude* (pp. 83–118). Rowley, MA: Newbury House.

Carroll, J.B. and Sapon, S.M. (1959) *Modern Language Aptitude Test*. San Antonio, TX: Psychological Corporation.

Celic, C. and Seltzer, K. (2011) *Translanguaging: A CUNY-NYSIEB Guide for Educators*. New York: CUNY-NYSIEB.

Cenoz, J. (2001) The effect of linguistic distance, L2 status and age on cross-linguistic influence in third language acquisition. In J. Cenoz, B. Hufeisen and U. Jessner (eds) *Cross-Linguistic Influence in Third Language Acquisition: Psycholinguistic Perspectives* (pp. 8–20). Clevedon: Multilingual Matters.

Cenoz, J. (2003) The additive effect of bilingualism on third language acquisition: A review. *International Journal of Bilingualism* 7 (1), 71–87.

Cenoz, J. (2004) Teaching English as a third language: The effect of attitudes and motivation. In C. Hoffmann and J. Ytsma (eds) *Trilingualism in Family, School and Community* (pp. 202–218). Clevedon: Multilingual Matters.

Cenoz, J. (2013) The influence of bilingualism on third language acquisition: Focus on multilingualism. *Language Teaching* 46 (1), 71–86.

Cenoz, J. and Valencia, J. (1994) Additive trilingualism: Evidence from the Basque Country. *Applied Psycholinguistics* 15, 197–209.

Cenoz, J. and Genesee, F. (1998) *Beyond Bilingualism: Multilingualism and Multilingual Education*. Clevedon: Multilingual Matters.

Cenoz, J. and Gorter, D. (2011) A holistic approach to multilingual education: Introduction. *The Modern Language Journal* 95 (3), 339–343.

Cenoz, J. and Gorter, D. (2017) Minority languages and sustainable translanguaging: Threat or opportunity? *Journal of Multilingual and Multicultural Development* 38, 901–912.

Cenoz, J. and Gorter, D. (2019) Minority languages, national state languages, and English in Europe: Multilingual education in the Basque Country and Friesland. *Journal of Multilingual Education Research* 9 (1), 9.

Chow, P. and Cummins, J. (2003) Valuing multilingual and multicultural approaches to learning. In S.R. Schecter and J. Cummins (eds) *Multilingual Education in Practice: Using Diversity as a Resource* (pp. 32–61). Portsmouth, NH: Heinemann.

Clyne, M. (2003) *Dynamics of Language Contact: English and Immigrant Languages*. Cambridge: Cambridge University Press.

Cook, V. (1991) The poverty of the stimulus argument and multicompetence. *Second Language Research* 7 (2), 103–117.

Cook, V. (1992) Evidence for multicompetence. *Language Learning* 42 (4), 557–592.

Cook, V. (1997) The consequences of bilingualism and cognitive processing. In A.M.B. de Groot and J.F. Kroll (eds) *Tutorials in Bilingualism: Psycholinguistic Perspectives* (pp. 279–299). Mahwah, NJ: Erlbaum.

Cook, V. (ed.) (2003) *Effects of the Second Language on the First*. Clevedon: Multilingual Matters.

Cook, V. (2015) Premises of multi-competence. In V. Cook and Li, W. (eds) *The Cambridge Handbook of Linguistic Multi-Competence* (pp. 1–25). Cambridge: Cambridge University Press.

Coulmas, F. (1989) *The Writing Systems of the World*. Oxford: Basil Blackwell.

Council of Europe (2001) *Common European Framework of Reference for Languages: Learning, Teaching, Assessment*. Cambridge: Cambridge University Press. http://www.coe.int/t/dg4/linguistic/Source/Framework_EN.pdf (accessed November 2021).

Creese, A. and Blackledge, A. (2015) Translanguaging and identity in educational settings. *Annual Review of Applied Linguistic* 35, 20–35.

Cummins, J. (1976) The influence of bilingualism on cognitive growth: A synthesis of research findings and explanatory hypotheses. *Working Papers on Bilingualism* 9, 1–43.
Cummins, J. (1979) Linguistic interdependence and the educational development of bilingual children. *Review of Educational Research* 49, 222–251.
Cummins, J. (1981) The role of primary language development in promoting educational success for language minority students. In California State Department of Education (ed.) *Schooling and Language Minority Students: A Theoretical Framework* (pp. 3–49). Los Angeles, CA: California State University.
Cummins, J. (2014) To what extent are Canadian second language policies evidence-based? Reflections on the intersections of research and policy. *Frontiers in Psychology* 5. https://doi.org/10.3389/fpsyg.2014.00358.
Cummins, J. (2021) *Rethinking the Education of Multilingual Learners: A Critical Analysis of Theoretical Concepts*. Bristol: Multilingual Matters.
D'Angelo, F. and Sorace, A. (2022) The additive effect of metalinguistic awareness in third or additional language acquisition. *International Journal of Bilingual Education and Bilingualism*. https://doi./org/10.1080/13670050.2022.2064710.
Dahm, R. (2015) Developing cognitive strategies through pluralistic approaches. In G. De Angelis, U. Jessner and M. Kresic (eds) *Cross-Linguistic Influence and Multilingualism* (pp. 43–70). London: Bloomsbury.
De Angelis, G. (2007) *Third or Additional Language Acquisition*. Clevedon: Multilingual Matters.
De Angelis, G. (2014) A multilingual approach to analysing standardized test results: Immigrant primary school children and the role of languages spoken in a bi-/multilingual community. *Intercultural Education* 25 (1), 14–18.
De Angelis, G. (2021) *Multilingual Testing and Assessment*. Bristol: Multilingual Matters.
de Bot, K. (1992) A bilingual production model: Levelt's speaking model approach. *Applied Linguistics* 13 (1), 1–24.
de Bot, K. (2004) The multilingual lexicon: Modelling selection and control. *International Journal of Multilingualism* 1, 17–32.
de Bot, K. and Jaensch, C. (2015) What is special about L3 processing? *Bilingualism: Language and Cognition* 18 (2), 130–144.
de Bot, K., Lowie, W. and Verspoor, M.H. (2007) A dynamic systems theory approach to second language acquisition. *Bilingualism: Language and Cognition* 10 (1), 7–21.
De Graaf, R. (1997) The eXperanto experiment: Effects of explicit instruction on second language acquisition studies. *Second Language Acquisition* 19, 249–276.
De Keyser, R. (1995) Learning second language grammar rules: An experiment with a miniature linguistic system studies. *Second Language Acquisition* 17, 379–410.
De Keyser, R., Salaberry, R., Robinson, P. and Harrington, M. (2002) What gets processed in processing instruction? A commentary on Bill Van Patten's processing instruction: An update. *Language Learning* 52, 805–823.
Dewaele, J. M. (2001) Activation or inhibition? The interaction of L1, L2 and L3 on the language mode continuum. In J. Cenoz, B. Hufeisen and U. Jessner (eds) *Cross-Linguistic Influence in Third Language Acquisition: Psycholinguistic Perspectives* (pp. 69–89). Clevedon: Multilingual Matters.
Dienes, Z. (2004) Assumptions of subjective measures of unconscious mental states. *Journal of Consciousness Studies* 11 (9), 25–45.
Dienes, Z. (2008) *Understanding Psychology as a Science: An Introduction to Scientific and Statistical Inference*. Basingstoke: Palgrave Macmillan.
Doughty, C. and Williams, J. (1998) *Focus on Form in Classroom Second Language Acquisition*. Cambridge: Cambridge University Press.
Doughty, C., Campbell, S., Mislevy, M., Bunting, M., Bowles, A. and Koeth, T. (2010) Predicting near-native ability: The factor structure and reliability of Hi-LAB. In M.

Prior, Y. Watanabe and S. Lee (eds) *Selected Proceedings of the 2008 Second Language Research Forum* (pp. 10–31). Somerville, MA: Cascadilla Proceedings Project.

Douglas Fir Group (2016) A transdisciplinary framework for SLA in a multilingual world. *Modern Language Journal* 95, 339–343.

Duff, P.A. and Li, P.A. (2009) Indigenous, minority, and heritage language education in Canada: Policies, contexts, and issues. *The Canadian Modern Language Review / La revue canadienne des langues vivantes* 66, 1–8.

Eckert, P. and McConnell-Ginet, S. (1995) Constructing meaning, constructing selves: Snapshots of language, gender and class from Belten High. In P. Eckert and J. Rickford (eds) *Style and Sociolinguistic Variation* (pp. 119–126). Cambridge: Cambridge University Press.

Edwards, J. (2004) Foundations of bilingualism. In T. Bhatia and W. Ritchie (eds) *The Handbook of Bilingualism* (pp. 7–31). Oxford: Blackwell.

El Euch, S. (2010) Attitudes, motivations et conscience métalinguistique chez des bilingues et des trilingues adultes: effets, similarités et différences. *Language Awareness* 19 (1), 17–33.

El Euch, S. (2011) Language aptitude and metalinguistic awareness in bilingual and in trilingual undergraduates. Paper presented at the Seventh Conference on Third Language Acquisition and Multilingualism, Warsaw (Poland), 15–17 September.

El Euch, S. and Huot, A. (2015) Strategies to develop metalinguistic awareness in adult learners. WEFLA 2015, International Conference on Foreign Languages, Communication and Culture, Holguin (Cuba), 27–29 April.

Ellis, E. (2013) The ESL teacher as plurilingual. An Australian perspective. *TESOL Quarterly* 47 (3), 446–471.

Ellis, N. (2002) Frequency effects in language acquisition: A review with implications for theories of implicit and explicit language acquisition. *Studies in Second Language Acquisition* 24, 143–188.

Ellis, N. (2011) Implicit and explicit SLA and their interface. In C. Sanz and R. Leow (eds) *Implicit and Explicit Language Learning: Conditions, Processes, and Knowledge in SLA and Bilingualism* (pp. 35–47). Washington, DC: Georgetown University Press.

Ellis, R. (1994) Implicit/explicit knowledge and language pedagogy. *TESOL Quarterly* 28, 166–172.

Ellis, R. (2005) Measuring implicit and explicit knowledge of a second language. *Studies in Second Language Acquisition* 27, 141–172.

Escobar, C.F. (2016) Challenging the monolingual bias in EFL programs: Towards a bilingual approach to L2 learning. *Revista de Lengus Modernas* 24, 249–266.

Ettlinger, M., Morgan-Short, K., Faretta-Stutenberg, M. and Wong, P.C. (2015) The relationship between artificial and second language learning. *Cognitive Science* 40 (4), 822–847.

European Centre for Modern Languages (2017) Teacher education for linguistic diversity: The contribution of the ECML. ECML Colloquium, 13–14 December 2017.

European Commission (2007) *Final Report: High Level Group on Multilingualism*. Luxembourg: European Communities. http://ec.europa.eu/education/policies/lang/doc/multireport_en.pdf.

European Commission, Directorate-General for Education, Youth, Sport and Culture (1996) *White Paper on Education and Training: Teaching and Learning: Towards the Learning Society*. Brussels: Commission of the European Communities.

Faerch, C. and Kasper, G. (1983) Plans and strategies in foreign language communication. In C. Faerch and G. Kasper (eds) *Strategies in Interlanguage Communication* (pp. 20–60). London: Longman.

Falk, Y. and Bardel, C. (2010) The study of the role of the background languages in third language acquisition: The state of the art. *IRAL* 48 (2–3), 185–219.

Falk, Y. and Bardel, C. (2011) Object pronouns in German L3 syntax: Evidence for the L2 status factor. *Second Language Research* 27 (1), 59–82.

Fehling, S. (2008) *Language Awareness und bilingualer Unterricht. Eine komparative Studie*. Frankfurt am Main: Peter Lang.

Fishman, J. (1966) The implication of bilingualism for language teaching and language learning. In A. Valdman (ed.) *Trends in Language Teaching* (pp. 146–158). New York: McGraw-Hill.

Flege, J., Mackay, I. and Piske, T. (2002) Assessing bilingual dominance. *Applied Psycholinguistics* 23, 567–598.

Flynn, S., Foley, C. and Vinnitskaya, I. (2004) The cumulative-enhancement model for language acquisition: Comparing adults' and children's patterns of development in first, second and third language acquisition of relative clauses. *The International Journal of Multilingualism* 1, 3–16.

Ford, J.D. and Ford, L.W. (1994) Logics of identity, contradiction, and attraction in change. *Academy of Management Review* 19, 756–785.

Fuchs, C. (1982) *La paraphrase*. Paris: Presse Universitaire de France.

Gabryś-Barker, D. (2012) *Reflectivity in Pre-Service Teacher Education: A Survey of Theory and Practice*. Katowice: Wydawnictwo Uniwersytetu Śląskiego.

Gabryś-Barker, D. (2019) Developing language awareness through students' conceptualisations: Metaphoric approach in content courses. In D. Gabryś-Barker (ed.) *Challenges of Foreign Language Instruction in the University Context* (pp 107–126). Katowice: Wydawnictwo Uniwersytetu Śląskiego.

Gallardo del Puerto, F. (2007) Is L3 phonological competence affected by the learner's level of bilingualism? *International Journal of Multilingualism* 4, 1–16.

García, O. (2005) Positioning heritage languages in the United States. *Modern Language Journal* 89 (4), 601–605.

García, O. (2009) *Bilingual Education in the 21st Century: A Global Perspective*. Malden, MA: Wiley Blackwell.

García, O. (2011) The translanguaging of Latino kindergarteners. In K. Potowski and J. Rothman (eds) *Bilingual Youth: Spanish in English Speaking Societies* (pp. 33–55). Amsterdam: John Benjamins.

García, O. (2020) Singularity, complexities and contradictions: A commentary about translanguaging, social justice, and education. In J. Panagiotopoulou. L. Rosen and J. Strzykala (eds) *Inclusion, Education and Translanguaging. Inklusion und Bildung in Migrationsgesellschaften* (pp. 11–20). Wiesbaden: Springer.

García, O. and Kano, N. (2014) Translanguaging as process and pedagogy: Developing the English writing of Japanese students in the US. In J. Conteh and G. Meier (eds) *The Multilingual Turn in Languages Education: Opportunities and Challenges* (pp. 258–277). Bristol: Multilingual Matters.

García, O. and Li, W. (2014) *Translanguaging: Language, Bilingualism and Education*. London: Palgrave Macmillan.

García, O. and Li, W. (2015) Translanguaging, bilingualism and bilingual education. In W. Wright, S. Boun and O. García (eds) *Handbook of Bilingual Education* (pp. 223–240). Malden, MA: John Wiley.

García, O., Flores, N. and Woodley, H. (2012) Transgressing monolingualism and bilingual dualities: Translanguaging pedagogies. In A. Yiakoumetti (ed.) *Harnessing Linguistic Variation for Better Education* (pp. 45–75). Bern: Peter Lang.

Gardner, R.C. (2001) Integrative motivation and second language acquisition. In Z. Dörnyei and R. Schmidt (eds) *Motivation and Second Language Acquisition* (pp. 1–19). Honolulu, HI: University of Hawaii Press.

Gathercole, V.C.M., Thomas, E.M., Roberts, E.J., Hughes, C.O. and Hughes, E.K. (2013) Why assessment needs to take exposure into account: Vocabulary and grammatical abilities in bilingual children. In V.C.M. Gathercole (ed) *Issues in the Assessment of Bilinguals* (pp. 20–55). Bristol: Multilingual Matters.

Genesee, F. and Lambert, W.E. (1983) Trilingual education for majority-language children. *Child Development* 54 (1), 105–114.

Gibson, M., Hufeisen, B. and Libben, G. (2001) Learners of German as an L3 and their production of German prepositional verbs. In J. Cenoz, B. Hufeisen and U. Jessner (eds) *Cross-linguistic Influence in Third Language Acquisition: Psycholinguistic Perspectives* (pp. 138–148). Clevedon: Multilingual Matters.

Giddens, A. (1991) *Modernity and Self-Identity; Self and Society in the Late Modern Age.* Cambridge: Polity Press.

Göbel, K. and Vieluf, S. (2014) The effects of language transfer as a resource in instruction. In P. Grommes and A. Hu (eds) *Plurilingual Education: Policies – Practice – Language Development* (pp. 181–195). Amsterdam: John Benjamins.

Gollan, T., Montoya, R.I., Cera, C. and Sandoval, T.C. (2008) More use almost always means a smaller frequency effect: Aging, bilingualism, and the weaker links hypothesis. *Journal of Memory and Language* 58, 787–814.

González-Alonso, J.G. and Rothman, J. (2017) Coming of age in L3 initial stages transfer models: Deriving developmental predictions and looking towards the future. *International Journal of Bilingualism* 21 (6), 683–697.

González-Alonso, J.G., Rothman, J., Berndt, D., Castro, T. and Westergaard, M. (2016) Broad scope and narrow focus: On the contemporary linguistic and psycholinguistic study of third language acquisition. *International Journal of Bilingualism* 21 (6), 639–650.

Green, D. (1986) Control, activation and resource. *Brain and Language* 27, 210–223.

Green, D. (1998) Mental control of the bilingual lexico-semantic system. *Bilingualism: Language and Cognition* 1, 67–81.

Grey, S., Sanz, C., Morgan-Short, K. and Ullman, M.T. (2018) Bilingual and monolingual adults learning an additional language: ERPs reveal differences in syntactic processing. *Bilingualism: Language and Cognition* 21, 970–994.

Griva, E., Panayiotis, P. and Nihoritou, I. (2016) Policies for plurilingual education and FL teaching in three European countries: A comparative account of teachers' views. *International Journal of Languages Education* 4 (2), 37–58.

Grosjean, F. (1985) The bilingual as a competent but specific speaker-hearer. *Journal of Multilingual Multicultural Development* 6, 467–477.

Grosjean, F. (1992) Another view of bilingualism. In R.J. Harris (ed.) *Advances in Psychology. Cognitive Processing in Bilinguals* (pp. 51–62). Oxford: North-Holland.

Grosjean, F. (1997) Processing mixed language: Issues findings and models. In A.M. De Groot and J.F. Kroll (eds) *Tutorials in Bilingualism* (pp. 225–254). Mahwah, NJ: Erlbaum.

Grosjean, F. (1998) The on-line processing of speech: Lexical access in bilinguals. In P. Bhatt and R. Davis (eds) *The Linguistic Brain* (pp. 3–12). Toronto, ON: Canadian Scholars' Press.

Grosjean, F. (2001) The bilingual's language modes. In J. Nicol (ed.) *One Mind, Two Languages: Bilingual Language Processing* (pp. 1–22). Oxford: Blackwell.

Grosjean, F. (2014) Myths about bilingualism. http://www.francoisgrosjean. ch/myths_en .htm (accessed 14 November 2021).

Gutiérrez, K.D. (2008) Developing a sociocritical literacy in the third space. *Reading Research Quarterly* 43 (2), 148–164. https://doi.org/10.1598/RRQ.43.2.3.

Haim, O. (2014) Factors predicting academic success in second and third language among Russian-speaking immigrant students studying in Israeli schools. *International Journal of Multilingualism* 11, 41–61.

Hakuta, K. (1986) Cognitive development of bilingual children. *Center for Language Education and Research Educational Report.* Los Angeles, CA: UCLA.

Hall, J.K. (2019) The contributions of conversation analysis and interactional linguistics to a usage-based understanding of language: Expanding the transdisciplinary framework. *The Modern Language Journal* 103, 80–94.

Harris, R. (1998) *Introduction to Integrational Linguistics*. Oxford: Pergamon.
He, A. (2006) Toward an identity theory of the development of Chinese as a heritage language. *Heritage Language Journal* 4 (1), 1–28.
He, A. (2010) The heart of heritage: Sociocultural dimensions of heritage language learning. *Annual Review of Applied Linguistics* 30, 66–82.
Hélot, C. and Young, A. (2006) Imagining multilingual education in France: A language and cultural awareness project at primary level. In O. García, T. Skutnabb-Kangas and M.E. Torres-Guzmán (eds) *Imagining Multilingual Schools: Languages in Education and Glocalization* (pp. 69–90). Clevedon: Multilingual Matters.
Herdina, P. and Jessner, U. (2002) *A Dynamic Model of Multilingualism: Perspectives of Change in Psycholinguistics*. Clevedon: Multilingual Matters.
Hernandez, A.E. and Li, P. (2007) Age of acquisition: Its neural and computational mechanisms. *Psychological Bulletin* 133, 638–650.
Hornberger, N.H. and Wang, S.C. (2008) Who are our heritage language learners?. In D. Brinton, O. Kagan and S. Bauckus (eds) *Heritage Language Education: A New Field Emerging* (pp. 3–35). New York: Routledge.
Huang, C.T. J. (2016) The syntax and semantics of prenominals: Construction or composition? *Language and Linguistics* 17, 431–475.
Huang, T., Loerts, H. and Steinkrauss, R. (2022) The impact of second- and third-language learning on language aptitude and working memory. *International Journal of Bilingual Education and Bilingualism* 25 (2), 522–538.
Hudelson, S. (1987) The role of native language literacy in the education of language minority children. *Language Arts* 64, 827–841.
Hufeisen, B. (1998) L3 – Stand der Forschung – Was bleibt zu tun? In B. Hufeisen and B. Lindemann (eds) *Tertiärsprachen: Theorien, Modelle, Methoden* (pp. 169–183). Tübingen: Stauffenburg Verlag.
Hufeisen, B. and Neuner, G. (eds) (2003) *Mehrsprachigkeitskonzept - Tertiärsprachen - Deutsch nach Englisch*. Strasbourg: Council of Europe.
Hulstijn, J.H. (2003) Connectionist models of language processing and the training of listening skills with the aid of multimedia software. *Computer Assisted Language Learning* 16, 413–425.
International Test Commission (2019) ITC guidelines for the large-scale assessment of linguistically diverse populations. *International Journal of Testing* 19 (4), 301–366.
Ivanova, I. and Costa, A. (2008) Does the bilingualism hamper lexical access in speech production? *Acta Psychologica* 127, 277–288.
Jaensch, C. (2009) L3 enhanced feature sensitivity as a result of higher proficiency in the L2. In Y-K.I. Leung (ed.) *Third Language Acquisition and Universal Grammar* (pp. 115–143). Bristol: Multilingual Matters.
Jaensch, C. (2012) Acquisition of L3 German. In A. Amaro, S. Flynn and J. Rothman (eds) *Third Language Acquisition in Adulthood* (pp. 165–194). Philadelphia, PA: John Benjamins.
James, C. (1996) A cross-linguistic approach to language awareness. *Language Awareness* 4, 138–148.
Jessner, U. (1999) Metalinguistic awareness in multilinguals: Cognitive aspects of third language learning. *Language Awareness* 8 (3–4), 201–209.
Jessner, U. (2006) *Linguistic Awareness in Multilingualism: English as a Third Language*. Edinburgh: Edinburgh University Press.
Jessner U. (2008a) Teaching third languages: Findings, trends and challenges. *Language Teaching* 41, 15–56.
Jessner, U. (2008b) A DST model of multilingualism and the role of metalinguistic awareness. *The Modern Language Journal* 92, 270–283.
Jessner, U., Allgäuer-Hackl, U.E. and Hofer, U.E. (2016) Emerging multilingual awareness in educational contexts: From theory to practice. *The Canadian Modern Language Review / La revue canadienne des langues vivantes* 72, 157–182.

Jiménez, R.T., David, S., Fagan, K., Risko, V., Pacheco, M., Pray, L. and Gonzales, M. (2015) Using translation to drive conceptual development for students becoming literate in English as an additional language. *Research in the Teaching of English* 49 (3), 248–271.

Kano, N. (2010) Translanguaging as a process and pedagogical tool for Japanese students in an English writing course in New York. Doctoral dissertation, Teachers College, Columbia University.

Kanno, Y. and Norton, B. (2003) Imagined communities and educational possibilities: Introduction. *Journal of Language, Identity, and Education* 2 (4), 241–249.

Kecskes, I. (2010) Situation-bound utterances as pragmatic acts. *Journal of Pragmatics* 42 (11), 2889–2897.

Kellerman, E. (1983) Now you see it, now you don't. In S. Gass and L. Selinker (eds) *Language Transfer in Language Learning* (pp. 112–134). Rowley MA: Newbury House.

Kellerman, E. and Bialystok, E. (1997) On psychological plausibility in the study of communication strategies. In G. Kasper and E. Kellerman (eds) *Communication Strategies: Psycholinguistic and Sociolinguistic Perspectives* (pp. 31–48). London: Longman.

Kemp, C. (2001) Metalinguistic awareness in multilinguals: Implicit and explicit grammatical awareness and its relationship with language experience and language attainment. Unpublished PhD thesis, University of Edinburgh.

Kemp, C. (2007) Strategic processing in grammar learning: Do multilinguals use more strategies? *International Journal of Multilingualism* 4 (4), 241–261.

Khan, K.A., Aigerim, D. and Xueqing, Z. (2020) Motivation, strategy and attitude: Sustainable challenges in Chinese language acquisition in India. *Revista Argentina de Clínica Psicológica* 29 (5), 1048–1059.

Kinginger, C. (2008) Language learning in study abroad: Case studies of Americans in France. *Modern Language Journal* 92, 1–124.

Kiramba, L. (2017) Translanguaging in the writing of emergent multilinguals. *International Multilingual Research Journal* 11 (2), 115–130. https://doi.org/10.1080/19313152.2016.1239457.

Kirwin, D. (2020) Converting plurilingual skills into educational capital. *Learn: Journal of the Irish Support Association* 41, 35–55.

Klein, E.C. (1995) Second versus third language acquisition: Is there a difference? *Language Learning* 45 (3), 419–446.

Knapp-Potthoff, A. (1997) Interkulturelle Kommunikationsfähigkeit als Lernziel. In A. Knapp-Potthoff and M. Liedke (eds) *Aspekte interkultureller Kommunikationsfähigkeit* (pp. 181–217). München: Iudicium.

Krashen, S.D. (1982) *Principles and Practice in Second Language Acquisition*. Oxford: Pergamon.

Krashen, S.D. (2004) *The Power of Reading*. Portsmouth, Heinemann and Westport: Libraries Unlimited.

Kroll, J.F. (2017) The benefits of multilingualism to the personal and professional development of residents of the US. *Foreign Language Annals* 50 (2), 248–259.

Kroll, J.F. and Bialystok, E. (2013) Understanding the consequences of bilingualism for language processing and cognition. *Journal of Cognitive Psychology* 25 (5), 497–514.

Kucukali, E. (2021) Multilingual teachers, plurilingual approach and L3 acquisition: Interviews with multilingual teachers and their L3/L3+ students. In J. Pinto and N. Alexandre (eds) *Multilingualism and Third Language Acquisition: Learning and Teaching Trends*. Berlin: Language Science Press.

Lambert, W.E. (1974) Culture and language as factors in learning and education. In F.E. Aboud and R.D. Meade (eds) *Cultural Factors in Learning and Education* (pp. 91–122). Bellingham, WA: Western Washington State College.

Laufer, B. and Hulstijn, J.H. (2001) Incidental vocabulary acquisition in a second language: The construct of task-induced involvement. *Applied Linguistics* 22, 1–26.

Lawton, D. and Gordon, V. (1996) *Dictionary of Education*. London: Hodder & Stoughton.

Lazo, M.G., Pumfrey, P.D. and Peers, I.S. (1997) Metalinguistic awareness, reading and spelling: Roots and branches of literacy. *Journal of Research in Reading* 20, 85–104.

Leeman, J. (2014) Critical approaches to the teaching of Spanish as a local-foreign language. In M. Lacorte (ed.) *The Handbook of Hispanic Applied Linguistics* (pp. 275–292). New York: Routledge.

Leeman, J. (2015) Heritage language education and identity in the United States. *Annual Review of Applied Linguistics* 35, 100–119.

Levelt, W.J.M. (1989) *Speaking: From Intention to Articulation*. Cambridge, MA: MIT Press.

Lewis, G., Jones, B. and Baker, C. (2012a) Translanguaging: Developing its conceptualisation and contextualisation. *Educational Research and Evaluation* 18 (7), 655–670.

Lewis, G., Jones, G. and Baker, C. (2012b) Translanguaging: Origins and development from school to street and beyond. *Educational Research and Evaluation: An International Journal on Theory and Practice* 18 (7), 641–654.

Li, W. (2011) Moment analysis and translanguaging space: Discursive construction of identities by multilingual Chinese youth in Britain. *Journal of Pragmatics* 43, 1222–1235.

Li, W. (2016) Multi-competence and the translanguaging instinct. In V. Cook and Li, W. (eds) *The Cambridge Handbook of Multi-Competence* (pp. 533–543). Cambridge: Cambridge University Press.

Li, W. (2018) Translanguaging as a practical theory of language. *Applied Linguistics* 39, 9–30.

Linck, J.A. and Weiss, D.J. (2011) Working memory predicts the acquisition of explicit L2 knowledge. In C. Sanz and R.P. Leow (eds) *Implicit and Explicit Language Learning: Conditions, Processes, and Knowledge in SLA and Bilingualism* (pp. 101–114). Washington, DC: Georgetown University Press.

Linck, J.A., Osthus, P., Koeth, J.T. and Bunting, M.F. (2014) Working memory and second language comprehension and production: A meta-analysis. *Psychonomic Bulletin & Review* 21, 861–883.

Little, D. and Kirwin, D. (2018) Translanguaging as a key to educational success: The experience of one Irish primary school. In P. Van Avermaet, S. Slembrouck, K. Van Gorp, S. Sierens and K. Maryns (eds) *The Multilingual Edge of Education* (pp. 313–339). London: Palgrave Macmillan.

Little, D. and Kirwin, D. (2019) *Engaging with Linguistic Diversity*. London: Bloomsbury Academic.

Llama, R., Cardoso, W. and Collins, L. (2010) The influence of language distance and language status on the acquisition of L3 phonology. *International Journal of Multilingualism* 7, 39–57.

Lo Bianco, J. and Aronin, L. (eds) (2020) *Dominant Language Constellations: A New Perspective on Multilingualism*. Cham: Springer.

Long, M. (1991) Focus on form: A design feature in language teaching methodology. In K. de Bot, R. Ginsberg and C. Kramsch (eds) *Foreign Language Research in Cross-Cultural Perspective* (pp. 196–221). Cambridge: Cambridge University Press.

Long, M. (2006) *Problems in SLA*. Mahwah, NJ: Erlbaum.

MacIntyre, P.D., Clément, R., Dörnyei, Z. and Noels, K. (1998) Conceptualizing willingness to communicate in a L2: A situational model of L2 confidence and affiliation. *Modern Language Journal* 82 (4), 545–562.

Mägiste, E. (1984) Stroop tasks and dichotic translation: The development of interference patterns in bilinguals. *Journal of Experimental Psychology: Learning, Memory, and Cognition* 10 (2), 304–315.

Mägiste, E. (1986) Selected issues in second and third language learning. In J. Vaid (ed.) *Language Processing in Bilinguals: Psycholinguistic and Neurolinguistic Perspectives* (pp. 97–122). Hillsdale, NJ: Lawrence Erlbaum.

Makoni, S. and Pennycook, A. (2005) Disinventing and (re)constituting languages. *Critical Inquiry in Language Studies* 2 (3), 137–156.

Makoni, S. and Pennycook, A. (2007) *Disinventing and Reconstituting Languages*. Clevedon: Multilingual Matters.

Malakoff, M. (1992) Translation ability: A natural bilingual and metalinguistic skill. In R. Harris (ed.) *Cognitive Processing in Bilinguals* (pp. 515–530). Hillsdale, NJ: Lawrence Erlbaum.

Malakoff, M. and Hakuta, K. (1991) Translation skill and metalinguistic awareness in bilinguals. In E. Bialystok (ed.) *Language Processing in Bilingual Children* (pp. 141–166). Cambridge: Cambridge University Press. https://doi.org/10.1017/CBO9780511620652.009.

Marian, V., Blumenfeld, H. and Kaushanskaya, M. (2007) The Language Experience and Proficiency Questionnaire (LEAP-Q): Assessing language profiles in bilinguals and multilinguals. *Journal of Speech, Language, and Hearing Research* 50, 940–967.

Martin, K. and Ellis, N. (2012) The roles of phonological short-term memory and working memory in L2 grammar and vocabulary learning. *Studies in Second Language Acquisition* 34 (3), 379–413.

Martínez-García, M.T. and Arnold, P. (2020) Translanguaging strategies for teaching literature in a multicultural setting. In P.-A. Mather (ed) *Technology-enhanced Learning and Linguistic Diversity: Strategies and Approaches to Teaching Students in a 2nd or 3rd Language* (pp. 39–49). Bingley: Emerald Publishing Limited.

Mary, L. and Young, A.S. (2017) From silencing to translanguaging: Turning the tide to support emergent bilinguals in transition from home to pre-school. In B. Paulsrud, J. Rosén, B. Straszer and Å. Wedin (eds) *New Perspectives on Translanguaging and Education* (pp. 108–128). Bristol: Multilingual Matters.

Mary, L. and Young, A.S. (2021) 'To make headway you have to go against the flow': Resisting dominant discourses and supporting emergent bilinguals in a multilingual pre-school in France. In L. Mary, A.B. Krüger and A.S. Young (eds) *Migration, Multilingualism and Education: Critical Perspectives on Inclusion* (pp. 112–129). Bristol: Multilingual Matters.

May, S. (2014) *The Multilingual Turn: Implications for SLA, TESOL and Bilingual Education*. New York: Routledge.

McDonough, S. (2002) *Applied Linguistics in Language Education* (1st edn). London: Routledge.

McLaughlin, B. (1990) Restructuring. *Applied Linguistics* 11 (2), 113–128.

Meara, P. (2005) *Llama Language Aptitude Tests*. Swansea: Lognostics.

Meißner, F-J. (2004) Transfer und Transferieren: Anleitungen zum Interkomprehensionsunterricht. In H.G. Klein and D. Rutke (eds) *Neuere Forschungen zur Europäische Interkomprehension* (pp. 39–66). Aacher: Shanken.

Merikle, P.M., Smilek, D. and Eastwood, J.D. (2001) Perception without awareness: Perspectives from cognitive psychology. *Cognition* 79, 115–134.

Michael, E.B. and Gollan, T.H. (2005) Being and becoming bilingual: Individual differences and consequences for language production. In J.F. Kroll and A.M.B. de Groot (eds) *Handbook of Bilingualism: Psycholinguistic Approaches* (pp. 389–407). Oxford: Oxford University Press.

Michael-Luna, S. and Canagarajah, A. (2007) Multilingual academic literacies: Pedagogical foundations for code meshing in primary and higher education. *Journal of Applied Linguistics* 4 (1), 55–77.

Mißler, B. (1999) *Fremdsprachenforschung und Lernstrategien. Eine empirische Untersuchung*. Tübingen: Stauffenburg.

Mohanty, A.K. (2019) *The Multilingual Reality: Living with Languages*. Bristol: Multilingual Matters

Muguruza, B., Cenoz, J. and Gorter, D. (2020) Implementing translanguaging pedagogies in an English medium instruction course. *International Journal of Multilingualism* 1–16.
Müller-Lancé, J. (2003a) A strategy model of multilingual learning. In J. Cenoz, B. Hufeisen and U. Jessner (eds) *The Multilingual Lexicon* (pp. 117–132). Dordrecht: Kluwer.
Müller-Lancé, J. (2003b) Der Wortschatz romanischer Sprachen in Tertiärspracherwerb. Tübingen: Stauffenburg.
Norris, J. and Ortega, L. (2000) Effectiveness of L2 instruction: A research synthesis and quantitative meta-analysis. *Language Learning* 50, 417–528.
Norton, B. (2000) *Identity and Language Learning: Gender, Ethnicity and Educational Change*. Harlow: Pearson Education/Longman
Norton, B. (2001) Non-participation, imagined communities, and the language classroom. In M. Breen (ed.) *Learner Contributions to Language Learning: New Directions in Research* (pp. 159–171). London: Pearson.
Norton, B. (2005) Towards a model of critical language teacher education. *Language Issues* 17 (1), 12–17.
Norton, B. (2012) Identity and second language acquisition. In C.A. Chapelle (ed.) *The Encyclopedia of Applied Linguistics* (pp. 1–8). Chichester: Wiley.
O'Laoire, M. (2001) Balanced bilingual and L1-dominant learners of L3 in Ireland. In J. Cenoz, B. Hufeisen and U. Jessner (eds) *Looking Beyond Second Language Acquisition: Studies in Third Language Acquisition and Trilingualism* (pp. 153–160). Tübingen: Stauffenburg.
O'Laoire, M. (2004) From L2 to L3/L4: A study of learners' metalinguistic awareness after 13 years' study of Irish. *CLCS Occasional Paper* 65, Autumn.
Oller, D.K. and Eilers, R.E. (2002) *Language and Literacy in Bilingual Children*. Clevedon: Multilingual Matters.
Olson, D. (1991) Literacy and metalinguistic activity. In D. Olson and N. Torrence (eds) *Literacy and Orality* (pp. 251–270). Cambridge: Cambridge University Press.
Olson, D. (2016) *The Mind on Paper: Reading, Consciousness and Rationality*. Cambridge: Cambridge University Press.
Ortega, L. (2009) *Understanding Second Language Acquisition*. London: Hodder Education.
Ortega, L. (2019) SLA and the study of equitable multilingualism. *The Modern Language Journal* 103, 23–38. https://doi.org/10.1111/modl.12525.
Otheguy, R., García, O. and Reid, W. (2015) Clarifying translanguaging and deconstructing named languages: A perspective from linguistics. *Applied Linguistics Review* 6 (3), 281–307.
Otheguy, R., García, O. and Reid, W. (2019) A translanguaging view of the linguistic system of bilinguals. *Applied Linguistics Review* 10 (4), 625–651.
Otsuji, E. and Pennycook, A. (2009) Metrolingualism: Fixity, fluidity and language in flux. *International Journal of Multilingualism* 7 (3), 240–254.
Otwinowska-Kasztelanic, A. (2011) Awareness of cognate vocabulary and vocabulary learning strategies of Polish multilingual and bilingual advanced learners of English. In J. Arabski and A. Wojtaszek (eds) *Individual Learner Differences in SLA* (pp. 110–126). Bristol: Multilingual Matters.
Otwinowska-Kasztelanic, A. (2014) Does multilingualism influence plurilingual awareness of Polish teachers of English? *International Journal of Multilingualism* 11 (1), 26–34.
Oxford, R. (1990) *Language Learning Strategies: What Every Teacher Should Know*. New York: Harper Collins.
Paap, K.R. and Greenberg, Z.I. (2013) There is no coherent evidence for a bilingual advantage in executive processing. *Cognitive Psychology* 66 (2), 232–258.
Paradis, M. (1994) Neurolinguistic aspects of implicit and explicit memory: Implications for bilingualism. In N. Ellis (ed.) *Implicit and Explicit Learning of Second Languages* (pp. 393–419). London: Academic Press.

Paradis, M. (2008) Language and communication disorders in multilinguals. In B. Stemmer and H. Whitaker (eds) *Handbook of the Neuroscience of Language* (pp. 341–349). Amsterdam: Elsevier.

Park, M. and Starr, R.L. (2016) The role of formal L2 learning experience in L3 acquisition among early bilinguals. *International Journal of Multilingualism* 13 (3), 271–291.

Peal, E. and Lambert, W. (1962) The relation of bilingualism to intelligence. *Psychological Monographs* 76 (546), 1–23.

Pennycook, A. (2010) *Language as a Local Practice*. London: Routledge.

Petitto, L.A., Berens, M.S., Kovelman, I., Dubins, M.H., Jasinska, K. and Shalinsky, M. (2012) The 'Perceptual Wedge Hypothesis' as the basis for bilingual babies' phonetic processing advantage: New insights from fNIRS brain imaging. *Brain and Language* 121, 130–143.

Pfenninger, S.E. and Singleton, D. (2016) Affect trumps age: A person-in-context relational view of age and motivation in SLA. *Second Language Research* 32, 1–35.

Pimsleur, P. (1966) *Pimsleur Language Aptitude Battery*. New York: Harcourt Brace Jovanovich.

Pinto, M.A. and El Euch, S. (2015) *La conscience métalinguistique: théorie, développement et instruments de mesure*. Québec: Presses de l'Université Laval.

Pinto, M.A., Titone, R. and Trusso, F. (1999) *Metalinguistic Awareness: Theory, Development and Measurement Instruments*. Rome: Istituti Editoriali e Poligrafici Internazionali.

Pittman, I. (2008) Bilingual and trilingual code-switching between Hungarian, Romanian and English in the speech of two Transylvanians living in North America. *International Journal of Multilingualism* 5, 122–139.

Portolés Falomir, L. (2014) Analysing prospective teachers' attitudes towards three languages in two different sociolinguistic and educational settings. In A. Otwinowska and G. De Angelis (eds) *Teaching and Learning in Multilingual Contexts: Sociolinguistic and Educational Perspectives* (pp. 50–74). Bristol: Multilingual Matters.

Poulisse, N., Bongaerts, T. and Kellerman, E. (1987) The use of retrospective verbal reports in the analysis of compensatory strategies. In C. Faerch and G. Kasper (eds) *Introspection in Second Language Research* (pp. 213–229). Clevedon: Multilingual Matters.

Puig-Mayenco, E., Cunnings, I., Bayram, F., Miller, D., Tubau, S. and Rothman, J. (2018) Language dominance affects bilingual performance and processing outcomes in adulthood. *Frontiers in Psychology* 9, 1199. https://doi.org/10.3389/fpsyg.2018.01199.

Raud, N. and Orehhova, O. (2020) Training teachers for multilingual primary schools in Europe: Key components of teacher education curricula. *International Journal of Multilingualism* 19 (1), 50–62.

Reber, A. (1967) Implicit learning of artificial grammars. *Journal of Verbal Learning and Verbal Behavior* 6 (6), 317–327.

Reber, A. (1993) *Implicit Learning and Tacit Knowledge: An Essay on the Cognitive Unconscious*. Oxford: Oxford University Press.

Rebuschat, P. (ed.) (2015) *Implicit and Explicit Learning of Languages*. Amsterdam: John Benjamins.

Rebuschat, P. and Williams, J. (2012) Implicit and explicit knowledge in second language acquisition. *Applied Psycholinguistics* 33 (4), 829–856.

Ringbom, H. (2001) Lexical transfer in L3 production. In J. Cenoz, B. Hufeisen and U. Jessner (eds) *Cross-Linguistic Influence in Third Language Acquisition: Psycholinguistic Perspectives* (pp. 59–68). Clevedon: Multilingual Matters.

Rivers, W.P. and Golonka, E.M. (2009) Third language acquisition Theory and practice. In M.H. Long and C.J. Doughty (eds) *The Handbook of Language Teaching* (pp. 250–266). Chichester: Blackwell Publishing.

Rizzi, L. (2004) On the study of the language faculty: Results, developments, and perspectives. *The Linguistic Review* 21, 323–344.

Robinson, P. (1997) Individual differences and the fundamental similarity of implicit and explicit adult second language learning. *Language Learning* 47, 45–99.

Robinson, P. (2002) *Individual Differences and Instructed Language Learning*. Amsterdam: John Benjamins.

Robinson, P. (2005) Aptitude and second language acquisition. *Annual Review of Applied Linguistics* 25, 46–73.

Robinson, P. (2011) Task-based language learning: A review of issues. *Language Learning* 61, 1–36.

Robinson, P. (2017) Attention and awareness. In J. Cenoz, D. Gorter and S. May (eds) *Language Awareness and Multilingualism* (pp. 125–134). Cham: Springer.

Robinson, P., Mackey, A., Gass, S. and Schmidt, R. (2012) Attention and awareness in second language acquisition. In S. Gass and A. Mackey (eds) *The Routledge Handbook of Second Language Acquisition* (pp. 247–267). New York: Routledge.

Roehr, K. (2008) Metalinguistic knowledge and language ability in university-level L2 learners. *Applied Linguistics* 29 (2), 173–199.

Roth, F.P., Speece, D.L., Cooper, D.H. and Paz, S.D.L. (1996) Unresolved mysteries: How do metalinguistic and narrative skills connect with early reading? *The Journal of Special Education* 30 (3), 257–277.

Rothman, J. (2010) On the typological economy of syntactic transfer: Word order and relative clause high/low attachment preference in L3 Brazilian Portuguese. *IRAL* 48 (2–3), 245–273.

Rothman, J. (2011) L3 syntactic transfer selectivity and typological determinacy: The typological primacy model. *Second Language Research* 27 (1), 107–127.

Rothman, J. (2015) Linguistic and cognitive motivations for the typological primacy model of third language (L3) transfer: Timing of acquisition and proficiency considered. *Bilingualism: Language and Cognition* 18 (2), 179–190.

Rothman, J. and Guijarro-Fuentes, P. (2012) Linguistic interfaces and language acquisition in childhood: Introduction to the special issue. *First Language* 32 (1–2), 3–16.

Sagasta Errasti, M.P. (2003) Acquiring writing skills in a third language: The positive effects of bilingualism. *The International Journal of Bilingualism* 7, 27–42.

Sanz, C. (2000) Bilingual education enhances third language acquisition: Evidence from Catalonia. *Applied Psycholinguistics* 21 (1), 23–44.

Sayer, P. (2013) Translanguaging, TexMex, and bilingual pedagogy: Emergent bilinguals learning through the vernacular. *TESOL Quarterly* 47 (1), 63–88.

Schecter, S.R and Cummins, J. (eds) (2003) *Multilingual Education in Practice: Using Diversity as a Resource*. Portsmouth, NH: Heinemann.

Schmidt, R. (1990) The role of consciousness in second language learning. *Applied Linguistics* 11, 129–158.

Schmidt, R. (1994) Implicit learning and the cognitive unconscious of artificial grammars and SLA. In N. Ellis (ed.) *Implicit and Explicit Learning of Languages* (pp. 165–209). London: Academic Press.

Schmidt, R. (1995) Consciousness and foreign language learning: A tutorial on the role of attention and awareness. In R. Schmidt (ed.) *Attention and Awareness in Foreign Language Teaching and Learning* (pp. 1–64). Honolulu, HI: University of Hawai'i at Manoa.

Schmidt, R. (2001) Attention. In P. Robinson (ed.) *Cognition and Second Language Instruction* (pp. 3–32). Cambridge: Cambridge University Press.

Seel, N. (2012) Metacognition and learning. In N. Seel (ed.) *Encyclopedia of the Sciences of Learning* (pp. 2228–2231). Heidelberg: Springer.

Skehan, P. (2015) Foreign language aptitude and its relationship with grammar: A critical review. *Applied Linguistics* 36, 367–384.

Snow, R.E. (1987) Aptitude complexes. In R.E. Snow and M.J. Farr (eds) *Aptitude, Learning and Instruction* (pp. 13–59). Hillsdale, NJ: Lawrence Erlbaum.

Snow, R.E. (1994) Abilities in academic tasks. In R.J. Sternberg and R.K. Wagners (eds) *Mind in Context: Interactionist Perspectives on Human Intelligence* (pp. 3–37). Cambridge: Cambridge University Press.

Sorace, A. (2006) Gradience and optionality in mature and developing grammars. In G. Fanselow, C. Fery, M. Schlesewsky and R. Vogel (eds) *Gradience in Grammar: Generative Perspective* (pp. 106–123). Oxford: Oxford University Press.

Sorace, A. (2011) Cognitive advantages in bilingualism: Is there a 'bilingual paradox'? In P. Valore (ed.) *Multilingualism. Language, Power, and Knowledge* (pp. 335–358). Pisa: Edistudio.

Sorace, A. (2016) Language and cognition in bilingual production: The real work lies ahead. *Bilingualism: Language and Cognition* 19 (5), 895–896.

Sorace, A. and Filiaci, F. (2006) Anaphora resolution in near-native speakers of Italian. *Second Language Research* 22 (3), 339–368.

Sorace, A. and Serratrice, L. (2009) Internal and external interfaces in bilingual language development: Beyond structural overlap. *International Journal of Bilingualism* 13 (2), 195–210.

Swain, M., Lapkin, S., Rowen, N. and Hart, D. (1990) The role of mother tongue literacy in third language learning. *Language, Culture and Curriculum* 3 (1), 65–68.

Terrell, T.D. (1991) The role of grammar instruction in a communicative approach. *The Modern Language Journal* 75 (1), 52–63.

Thomas, J. (1988) The role played by metalinguistic awareness in second and third language learning. *Journal of Multilingual and Multicultural Development* 9, 235–247.

Ticheloven, A., Blom, E., Leseman, P. and McMonagle, S. (2019) Translanguaging challenges in multilingual classrooms: Scholar, teacher and student perspectives. *International Journal of Multilingualism* 18 (3), 491–514.

Tomlin, R.S. and Villa, V. (1994) Attention in cognitive science and second language acquisition. *Studies in Second Language Acquisition* 16, 183–203.

Török, V. and Jessner, U. (2017) Multilingual awareness in Ln (foreign language) learners strategies and processing. *Hungarian Journal of Applied Linguistics* 17 (2), 1–18.

Truscott, J. and Sharwood Smith, M. (2011) Input, intake, and consciousness: The quest for a theoretical foundation. *Studies in Second Language Acquisition* 33, 497–528.

Trybulec, M. (2021) Skillful use of symbolizations and the dual nature of metalinguistic awareness. *Language Sciences* 84 (1), 101356.

Valdés, G. (2001) Heritage languages students: Profiles and possibilities. In J.K. Peyton, D.A. Ranard and S. McGinnis (eds) *Heritage Languages in America: Preserving a National Resource* (pp. 37–77). Washington, DC: Center for Applied Linguistics/Delta Systems.

Valdés, G. (2005) Bilingualism, heritage language learners, and SLA research: Opportunities lost or seized? *The Modern Language Journal* 89 (3), 410–426.

Valdés, G. and Figueroa, R.A. (1994) *Bilingualism and Testing: A Special Case of Bias*. New York: Ablex Publishing.

Varga, S. (2021) The relationship between reading skills and metalinguistic awareness. *Gradus* 8 (1), 52–57.

Werker, J.F. (1986) The effect of multilingualism on phonetic perceptual flexibility. *Applied Psycholinguistics* 7, 141–156.

Westney P. and Odlin T. (1994) Rules and pedagogical grammar. In T. Odlin (ed.) *Perspectives on Pedagogical Grammar* (pp. 72–99). Cambridge: Cambridge University Press.

Williams, C. (1994) Arfarniad o Ddulliau Dysgu ac Addysgu yng Nghyd-destun Addysg Uwchradd Ddwyieithog [An evaluation of teaching and learning methods in the context of bilingual secondary education]. Unpublished doctoral thesis, University of Wales.

Williams, C. (1996) Secondary education: Teaching in the bilingual situation. In C. Williams, G. Lewis and C. Baker (eds) *The Language Policy: Taking Stock* (pp. 39–78). Llangefni: CAI Language Studies Centre.

Williams, C. (2000) Welsh-medium and bilingual teaching in the further education sector. *International Journal of Bilingual Education and Bilingualism* 3 (2), 129–148.

Williams, C. (2002) *Ennill iaith: Astudiaeth o Sefyllfa Drochi yn 11-16 oe [A Language Gained: A Study of Language Immersion at 11-16 Years of Age]*. Bangor: School of Education.

Williams, C. (2012) *The National Immersion Scheme Guidance for Teachers on Subject Language Threshold: Accelerating the Process of Reaching the Threshold* (manuscript). Bangor: The Welsh Language Board.

Yelland, G.W., Pollard, J. and Mercuri, A. (1993) The metalinguistic benefits of limited contact with a second language. *Applied Psycholinguistics* 14, 423–444.

Ziegler, G. (2013) Multilingualism and the language education landscape: Challenges for teacher training in Europe. *Multilingual Education* 3, 1–23.

Zipke, M. (2008) Teaching metalinguistic awareness and reading comprehension with riddles. *Reading Teacher* 62 (2), 128–137.

Index

acquisition process, 1, 43, 52, 100, 128
additional language acquisition, 1, 10, 12, 21–22, 32–33, 43, 56–77, 100, 128, 133
additional language learning, 2, 4, 10, 12, 14, 54–56, 64–65, 71, 75, 77–78, 108–9, 124, 126–27
additive bilingualism, 4, 79, 89, 96–97, 99
applied linguistics, 10, 28, 33, 49, 80, 132–33, 137–41, 143–44
approaches, methodological, 32, 54, 126
aptitude, 37–40, 81
Aronin, L., 15, 59, 101, 109, 112, 130, 139
artificial grammars, 66–67, 142–43
assessment, 5–6, 10, 102–4, 107–8, 111, 132–33, 135
assessment strategies, 102
assessment tools, 5, 102, 107
attitudes, 33, 40–43, 46, 54, 110, 112, 121, 132, 134, 138, 142
awareness, 22, 24, 47, 49, 56–58, 61–66, 71–72, 77, 121, 126, 140, 143

Bialystok, E., 2, 8, 35–36, 57–58, 63, 67–68, 76, 131, 138, 140
bilingual advantage, 8–9, 33, 43–44, 52, 54, 141
bilingual children, 9, 14, 35, 131, 133, 135–36, 140–41
bilingual education, 43, 89–90, 93, 131, 133, 135, 137, 140, 143–44
bilingualism, 1–4, 6–7, 9, 11–15, 29–31, 33–36, 43–46, 51–54, 57–58, 62–63, 67–69, 78, 89–90, 97–98, 126–27, 130–44
  dynamic, 89–90
  early, 54, 62–63

bilingual language processing, 8–9, 69, 136
bilingual learners, 1, 6, 12, 28, 55, 58, 76, 78, 94
bilinguals, 1–3, 8–12, 14–15, 25, 31, 33–38, 43–44, 52–55, 57–59, 62–63, 66–68, 75–78, 87–88, 90, 101–27, 134–36, 139–42
bilinguals and multilinguals, 10, 25, 87, 109, 140
bilingual speech production models, 15–17
biliteracy, 51–52, 98, 114
biliteracy and bilingualism, 51, 114

Canagarajah, S., 83, 88, 119, 131, 140
CEM (Cumulative Enhancement Model), 7, 21, 23–24, 32
Cenoz, J., 1–2, 7, 13–14, 20, 53, 57, 59, 62, 82, 85, 132–33, 136, 141–43
challenges, 2, 6, 61, 95, 111, 124–25, 128–30, 135, 137, 145
classroom, 83–84, 93, 95, 102, 105, 109–10, 113–15, 117–18, 120–21, 123–24, 128, 131
codes, 11, 71, 83, 99, 110, 127
code-switching, 4, 14, 17–18, 60, 79, 83–84, 95–98, 102, 142
cognition, 7, 19, 35, 37, 43, 57, 131, 133, 136, 138–40, 143–44
cognitive abilities, 7, 35, 38–40
cognitive processes, 38, 57, 63, 81, 131
cognitive strategies, 59, 133
cognitive tasks, 34, 37, 57
communication strategies, 60, 76, 138
contexts, 4, 11, 13, 15, 37, 39, 41, 72–73, 76–79, 83–85, 87–88, 90, 93, 103, 105–7

Cook, V., 13, 59, 87, 101–2, 130, 132, 139
crosslinguistic, 5, 97, 109, 113, 115–16, 124, 126, 128
crosslinguistic influence, 7, 17, 19–20, 32, 53, 83, 101
crosslinguistic interaction, 14, 29, 76–77
Cummins, J., 2, 44–45, 93, 96–98, 113, 115–16, 122, 132–33, 143
Cumulative Enhancement Model. *See* CEM

De Angelis, G., 3, 5, 10, 15–16, 19, 21, 34, 43, 102–6, 133, 142
development of MLA, 47, 52, 54, 56–58, 60, 63, 69–70, 72–73, 77, 109, 119
dichotomies, 71, 92, 97, 103
DLC (dominant language constellation), 15, 82, 130, 139
DMM (Dynamic Model of Multilingualism), 28–30, 56, 137
domains, cognitive, 8, 30, 63, 99
dominant language constellation. *See* DLC
DST (Dynamic System Theory), 4, 7, 14, 28–30, 79
Dynamic Model of Multilingualism. *See* DMM

education, formal, 87, 108
educational contexts, 1, 5, 42, 89, 91, 95, 101–2, 112, 127, 137
Educational Research, 130, 133, 139
education systems, 88, 92, 107, 115, 127
  monolingual, 99
  national, 91
effects of bilingualism, 7, 9, 14–15, 29, 45, 63
emergent bilinguals, 11, 90, 93–94, 118, 120, 140
environments, 39, 106, 108
evaluation, 124, 139, 144
executive control, 8, 37, 67–69, 131
experience, 20, 24, 43–44, 48, 53, 61, 67–68, 116, 123, 127, 131
explicit instruction, 4, 48–51, 127, 133
Explicit Language Learning, 46, 134, 139
explicit learning, 48, 50, 63, 141–43

exposure, 1, 4, 12, 33, 45–46, 54, 59, 86, 106, 108, 116

factors
  affective, 41–42
  cognitive, 20, 26, 31
  external, 1, 3, 6, 26, 33, 54, 78
  individual, 10, 13, 29, 35, 76
  linguistic, 26, 32, 58
Falk, Y., 22–23, 130, 134–35
Flynn, S., 7, 21–23, 135, 137
formal context, 3, 26, 33, 54, 58, 78

García, O. 14, 79–82, 89–97, 119–20, 135, 137, 141
grammar, 22–24, 28, 30, 44–45, 47–48, 58–59, 66, 101, 130–31, 140, 143
Grosjean, F. 3, 10, 13, 25, 28, 87–88, 136
growth, cognitive, 44, 78, 133

heritage language education, 88, 95, 134, 137
heritage language learners, 85–86, 137, 144
heritage languages. *See* HL
HL (heritage languages), 4, 42, 45, 51, 79, 85–87, 89, 95, 99, 137, 144
HL education, 88–89
holistic approach, 9–10, 12, 28–29, 32, 103, 111, 132
Hufeisen, B., 26–27, 61, 130, 132–33, 136–37, 141–42

identities, multicultural, 98, 120
Implicit and Explicit Language Learning, 134, 139
implicit learning, 48–50, 66, 143
inclusion, 45, 99, 113–14, 124, 128, 135, 140
individual differences, 37–38, 40, 131, 143
instruction, 1, 4, 45, 48–49, 61–62, 65–67, 78, 84, 103–4, 111, 113, 118–21, 123–24
instructional practices, 5, 113–14, 116, 121–22, 124, 128
interaction, 14–15, 17, 25, 32, 36, 40, 53, 59, 88, 92, 95

Jaensch, C., 2, 30, 45–46, 53, 62, 133, 137
Jessner, U., 2, 26–30, 33, 60–62, 75–77, 132–33, 136–37, 141–42, 144

Kemp, C., 52, 66, 69, 76–77, 138
knowledge
 background, 72, 114, 120
 implicit, 47–48, 50, 52, 63
Kroll, J., 8, 132, 136, 138, 140

L2 in L3, 53
Lambert, 34–35, 89, 136, 138, 142
language acquisition, 6, 9–10, 12–13, 21, 23, 26, 30, 33, 36, 39, 41–42, 47–49, 61, 111, 134–35
language and cognition, 19, 57, 131, 133, 136, 143–44
language awareness, 26, 60, 85, 113–16, 134–35, 137
language education, 6, 42, 85, 91, 109, 115, 135–36, 140
language knowledge, 19, 68, 101
language learners, 1–3, 11, 13, 40, 88, 126, 128
 additional, 14, 32, 54–55, 75, 92
language learning, 3–4, 6–9, 12–13, 37–38, 52–53, 58–59, 61–65, 67–68, 77–78, 88, 92–93, 108–9, 131–35, 137–38, 141, 143
language learning process, 16, 26, 37, 102, 109, 127
language mode continuum, 25–26, 133
language processing, 37, 81, 125, 137–38, 140
language repertoire, 15, 82, 101
languages and cultures, 116–17, 123–24
Language Teaching, 131–32, 135, 137, 142
learners, 4–5, 7–8, 12–15, 18, 20–22, 26–28, 30, 39, 41–42, 44–46, 48–50, 58–62, 65–66, 71–76, 89–90, 92–95, 102–3, 108–12, 118, 127–28
learning environments, 47, 53, 108
learning strategies, 2–3, 22, 26, 54, 61, 66, 75, 77, 93, 98, 100, 125, 128–29
level of MLA, 29, 71, 74–75, 77, 111
Levelt, W., 15, 17, 133, 139

lexical access, 8, 20, 35, 137
Li, W., 4, 80-81, 91–92, 95, 120, 130, 132, 134–35, 137, 139
linguistic awareness, 61, 77, 94, 103, 118–19
linguistic competence, 11, 44, 102, 112
linguistic diversity, 134, 139–40
linguistic inputs, 32, 66, 126
linguistic tasks, 37, 43, 100, 128
literacy, 4, 51–52, 54, 56, 60, 63, 68–71, 94, 98, 127, 131, 139, 141

memory, 8, 39, 43, 46, 64, 136, 139
metacognitive strategies, 28, 60, 71, 76
metalinguistic concepts, 4, 56–58
metalinguistic knowledge, 4, 22, 44, 47, 56, 58, 63, 74
metalinguistic skills, 7, 52, 71, 140
methods, 13, 103, 131
minority, 4, 10, 43, 51, 87, 91, 95, 122, 134
 linguistic, 42, 87
minority languages, 8, 41–42, 80, 84–87, 91, 99, 122, 124, 128, 132
MLA, 2–4, 29, 46–47, 49, 52–54, 56–63, 66–79, 92, 95, 108–9, 111–12, 119–21, 127
monolingual bias, 10–11, 13, 87, 95, 122, 124, 130, 134
monolinguals, 9, 12–15, 25, 31, 34–36, 38, 43, 45–46, 52, 55, 59, 62, 75
monolinguals and bilinguals, 9, 14–15, 31, 35, 68, 80, 122
motivation, 13, 26, 31, 37–38, 40–43, 45, 51, 132, 134, 138, 142
multicompetence, 15, 59, 101, 132
multicultural, 6, 124, 128
multilingual acquisition, 4, 6, 10, 19, 56, 79, 126
multilingual contexts, 5, 14, 42, 103, 105–6, 111, 113, 115, 128, 131, 142
multilingual education, 1–2, 4, 79–80, 99, 101–25, 130, 132, 143, 145
Multilingual Education, 79–99
multilingualism, 1, 3–4, 6–7, 14–15, 25, 28–30, 79–82, 84, 95–97, 99, 102, 109–11, 113, 126, 130–45

multilingual learners, 2, 4, 6, 26, 29, 76, 79, 81–82, 92, 95, 100–101, 109, 111, 124–25, 128–29
multilingual learning, 60, 65, 76, 141
multilingual repertoire, 7, 12–13, 20, 30–31, 78–79, 81, 83–84, 102, 115, 119
multilingual resources, 98, 110, 117
multilingual speakers, 6, 13, 19–20, 25, 29, 79, 82, 90, 98, 101, 103
multilingual students, 2, 111, 114, 121, 124
multilingual teachers, 109–11, 138

native speakers, 11, 47–48, 85, 89, 99, 105–6

Ortega, L., 37, 40–41, 84, 141

pedagogical approaches, 80, 122
Pennycook, 81, 88, 96–97, 140–42
perspectives, holistic, 1, 10, 55, 82, 102, 126
plurilingual approaches, 102, 108–11, 138
practices, educational, 92, 95, 100, 122, 124, 127
Prior Formal Language Learning, 33–55
processing, 6, 10, 19, 25, 30, 57, 60, 62, 64–66, 133, 136
process of TLA, 1, 13, 27, 32, 66, 75, 78, 83, 120
profiles, linguistic, 3, 55, 92
programmes, educational, 91, 99, 124, 128

Rebuschat, P., 63, 65, 142
repertoire, multicultural, 5, 117, 122, 124–25
Representation Analysis, 35, 54, 127
research on multilingualism, 25, 95, 102, 126
resources, multisemiotic, 128
Robinson, P., 39–40, 49, 63–64, 67, 133, 143
Rothman, J., 7, 19, 21, 23–24, 53, 131, 135–37, 142–43

Sanz, C., 52, 131, 134, 136, 139, 143
Schmidt, R., 50, 62, 65–67, 135, 143

school and community, 120, 130, 132
school contexts, 71, 85, 106, 113, 121, 127
schooling, 9, 69, 93–94, 99, 124, 133
school language, 95, 98, 114–15
Second Language Acquisition, 133–35, 138, 141, 143–44
Second Language Research, 130, 132, 135, 142–44
skills, 43, 46, 51, 60, 69, 73, 82, 94, 98, 108, 112
SLA (second language acquisition), 1–3, 6–7, 10, 12–14, 26–27, 32, 36–37, 48, 50, 61, 79, 126, 131, 133–35, 138–44
societies, 1, 42, 89, 121, 136
Sorace, A., 12, 30–31, 66, 133, 143–44
speech production, 6, 19, 32, 36, 137
strategies, 26–27, 68, 71–73, 75–77, 79, 82–83, 93–94, 110, 112, 127–28, 134, 138, 140

target language (TL), 1, 6, 12–13, 18–19, 21, 27–28, 35, 41, 53, 59, 76–77, 109–10
tasks, metalinguistic, 57, 68, 124
teachers, x–1, 41–42, 61, 71, 73, 89–90, 92, 94–95, 98–100, 102–4, 107, 109–14, 116–24, 128, 144–45
teacher training, 112, 130, 142, 145
teaching, 1, 60–61, 95, 97–98, 101–2, 111–13, 124–25, 128–29, 132, 134, 137–39, 142, 144
Teaching and Learning Third Languages, 1–144
teaching methods, 48, 111, 116, 123
teaching practices, 2, 53, 91, 102
tests, 5, 24, 34, 39, 45, 65–66, 68–69, 71, 74, 103–5, 118
third language acquisition. See TLA
Thomas, J., 3, 33, 62, 135, 144
Threshold Hypothesis, 9, 43, 45–46
TLA (third language acquisition), 1–4, 6–33, 42–45, 52–56, 59–60, 62, 65–68, 75–79, 82–83, 109, 117, 126–28, 130, 132–38, 141–43
TPM (Typological Primacy Model), 7, 21, 23–24, 32, 143

transfer, 13, 19–21, 23–25, 28, 32, 45, 50, 53, 97–98, 102, 140, 143
　source of, 20–24, 53–54
translanguaging, 2, 4–5, 14, 79–100, 113, 115, 117–21, 123–25, 127–28, 131–32, 135, 138–41, 143
translanguaging approach, 80–81, 84–85, 90, 95, 118–19, 127
translanguaging practices, 4, 85, 94–95, 118–19, 123
translation, 73, 76, 95, 114, 123, 138

Trilingualism, 130, 132, 141
typological proximity, 24, 51, 78

UG (Universal Grammar), 46, 137

Valdés, G., 86, 89, 144

Williams, 63, 84, 90, 96, 117–18, 133, 142, 144–45
WM (working memory), 9, 37–38, 52, 130–31, 137, 139–40

For Product Safety Concerns and Information please contact our EU Authorised Representative:

Easy Access System Europe

Mustamäe tee 50

10621 Tallinn

Estonia

gpsr.requests@easproject.com

www.ingramcontent.com/pod-product-compliance
Lightning Source LLC
Chambersburg PA
CBHW052050300426
44117CB00012B/2058